I may be
HOMELESS
but you should see my
YACHT

A Memoir

I may be HOMELESS *but you should see my* YACHT

A Memoir

by

Mama Lee Wachtstetter

with

Joe Kita

ISBN: 978-0692932568

This memoir is true to the best of my recollection.
If I've made any mistakes, they are not intentional.
I'm almost 90, for goodness sake!

Cover photos of Mama Lee by Paragon Pixels / Crystal Cruises

This book is dedicated to Mason, my loving, thoughtful and considerate husband of 50 years, who I still miss every day, and also to my daughter Cathy, the oldest of my four children, who was taken from us much too soon.

Thanks to all my friends and family members who have been so helpful and supportive during the writing of this book. Also to the staff and crew of the Crystal Serenity and the administration of Crystal Cruises, without whose cooperation this story could not be told. And a special thanks to Joe Kita, my friend and co-author.
Enjoy!

TABLE OF CONTENTS

INTRODUCTION

I Went Viral!

Shortly before the start of the 2015 World Cruise on the Crystal Serenity, an elderly gentleman approached me and introduced himself as a journalist. We chatted for a while on the Lido Deck, and he asked me lots of questions about what it's like living at sea. He wrote a short article that was eventually published in *USA Today*.

Over the years I've had lots of stories published about me in all kinds of newspapers and magazines. But this one got the most attention of all, no doubt because it discussed how much it costs me annually to live fulltime on a luxury cruise ship. Even though the figures were wrong, news outlets around the world picked up the story, and soon the Crystal public relations department started getting requests for interviews. These included *Good Morning America, UK Daily Mail, ABC News, CNBC, Fox Business, People Magazine, CBS, NBC, The Sharon Osbourne Show*, and many others.

It was crazy. I'd get back to my stateroom at the end of the day, and the little light would be blinking on my telephone. Once there was a message from a producer with *The Ellen DeGeneres Show*. She wanted to fly me to the studio, all expenses paid, to appear on the program with Ellen. How did she even get my number?

When the ship stopped in the Dominican Republic in mid-January, a group of local travel agents came aboard for a tour and lunch. This happens often in ports; it's a great way to familiarize agents with the ship so they can sell it better. But this time one of the "agents" was actually a reporter. She immediately started asking people, "Where is Mama Lee? Can I talk to her?" Well, some of the crew got suspicious, and the hotel director ended up throwing her off the ship. I never saw him so angry.

In March, a lecturer named Roman Pryjomko joined the ship. He told me he'd been sitting in the waiting room at a dental office in Krakow leafing through one of the Polish daily newspapers, when he spotted a big story about me. And later, when the ship reached Cape Town, someone brought me a copy of *People South Africa*. Beyoncé was on the cover, and inside was a story about me! I was glad that these articles didn't cast me as some eccentric old lady, but rather as an inspirational person living a vibrant life.

All this attention got me thinking that maybe it was time to write my memoir. Based on my cruising for nearly 60 years, visiting more than 100 countries, and living fulltime at sea for over a decade, people have been encouraging me to write for years. But I always doubted whether anyone would be interested in hearing my stories.

Now I know they are.

I hope you enjoy them, too.

Mama Lee
Aboard the Crystal Serenity
June 2017

Chapter 1

THE DAY THE SHIP CAUGHT FIRE

It was 1996, and I was aboard the Cunard Sagafjord with my husband, Mason. It was the 54th day of a 110-day World Cruise, and we were in the middle of the South China Sea. The cruise had been lovely up to this point. This was our first World Cruise. We had brought our 10-year-old granddaughter, Alecia, on the ship before departing. (This was back in the days when you didn't have all that security nonsense.) And as we were showing her around, she said, "Grandma, I just love the smell of luxury." I'd never heard that expression before; it was hilarious. But you know what? She was right, and we had been enjoying every minute of it.

But then disaster nearly struck.

It was 10 a.m., and Mason and I were sitting in one of the lounges waiting for a lecture to begin. I decided to go to the ladies room, so I wouldn't have to bother anyone once the lecture started. It was a very small ladies room. It held one person and, of course, there were no windows. So I sat down and, suddenly, the light went out and I was in total darkness. I felt like I was in a closet and someone had flipped off the switch. I was totally disoriented. I groped my way out of the stall and felt my way along the wall. The room was pitch black, and I had no idea where the door was. I remembered there was a single light bulb overhead, and I started getting really mad that no one had checked it. I mean, how difficult can it be to regularly change a light bulb? I finally found the door and yanked it open, but the hall was just as dark.

What's going on?

For some reason, an officer was standing just outside the door. As I was about to tell him off and complain about the light bulb being burned out, an announcement came on the public address system.

"Will all officers and crew please put on your life jackets immediately. We repeat, will all officers and crew please put on your life jackets immediately."

Oh how lovely, I thought, and then turning to the officer standing beside me, I asked, "What about the passengers?"

"Don't worry," he said. "If you need to put on a life jacket they will tell you."

I found my way back into the lounge and sat down next to Mason. Since there were windows in the room, there was enough light to get around. The lecture had never started because there was no electricity for the microphone. Everybody was wondering what was going on.

Although we didn't know it at the time, a fire was raging in the engine room. Fire at sea is the worst of all possible dangers. And at that very moment, the crew was trying to contain this one. It was so intense that I later learned groups of three or four firefighters would go in, battle the blaze for 15 or 20 minutes and then come out and slump exhausted against the wall while another group went in. It took three hours to get it under control, and all the ship's engines were destroyed.

But in the lounge and throughout the ship, none of the crew even uttered the word, "Fire." That was intentional. Hearing that word would have sparked panic among the 500 guests, and the crew knew it. In retrospect, it was actually handled beautifully. All the guests stayed calm, trusting in the staff although we were wondering what was going on.

Mason and I left the lounge and walked out on deck. That's when we saw smoke pouring from the ship's chimney and started to suspect what was happening. The black smoke was a stark contrast to the beautiful blue sky and smooth sea. Fortunately, this weather would hold for the next five days.

Once the fire was extinguished and the crisis had passed – although we still didn't know that – they opened the bars and our cruise suddenly became all-inclusive. Whatever fear and trepidation there might have been vanished quickly amidst unlimited refills of free alcoholic beverages. Everyone was drinking up a storm until several hours later when the ice ran out. Without any power, the ship could also not make any ice, which incidentally is the second worst of all possible dangers at sea on a cruise ship. Just as quickly as it began, the party wound down.

At some point during all this, the captain announced that everything was under control – still without using the word "fire" – and said Cunard's main London office had been notified and help would probably arrive by 6 p.m. Miraculously, only one guest had been hurt when the lights went off. Her heel caught in the carpet coming down the stairs, and she broke a few bones. Beyond that, everything seemed safe and secure. How frightened can you be in a situation where there's absolutely nothing you can do?

A more immediate problem for the guests was where our next meal would be coming from. With no electricity, the dining room had been locked. We never got to eat another meal in there. The crew set up grills around the pool and cooked and served meals on deck. They also had to carry the plates and supplies five stories up and then down the stairs from the kitchen because the elevators weren't working. The crew really went above and beyond to keep everyone happy. All of the dining-room waiters, who were now out of jobs, were assigned to anyone needing personal assistance. It was wonderful to see.

But having no electricity also meant no air-conditioning and no plumbing. Our cabin essentially became an outhouse. You could use the toilet but you couldn't flush. It was no picnic. The smell was so bad you couldn't stay in your room at all. At night, people took their linen, a blanket and a pillow, and slept on the lounge chairs around the pool (if you were lucky enough to get one) or on the deck itself.

Six p.m. came and went but there were no rescue ships or planes in sight. The next morning the captain said more of the same – everything was under control and help was on the way.

One thing Mason did immediately when we realized what had happened was go to the front desk and ask for the money we had put in the ship's safe. In those days, the staterooms didn't have those little safes in the closet like they do now. And these were also the days before credit cards, so you traveled with a significant amount of cash, especially on a World Cruise. If anything else happened to the ship, Mason wanted to be sure we had our cash. And they gave it to him, no questions asked.

The mood on the ship was fascinating to watch. Although we were adrift for three days, even the chronic complainers stopped complaining, and everyone became friends. We all realized how lucky we were. Even though the captain kept telling us each day that help would arrive by 6 p.m. and it never did, we didn't care. It was a lovely bonding experience. And this good mood became more noticeable with each passing day. Without any formal entertainment, our fellow passengers became the entertainment.

There was one performance, though. An opera singer was on board. Although there were no microphones, he didn't need any amplification. So one evening he sang for everyone around the pool, and his voice filled the whole sky.

Our ship's stranding was big news around the world, and everyone's families back home were worried. Cunard's main office responded reassuringly to all callers

Finally, on Day 3 two tugboats arrived to tow us to Manila. But unlike the ship, which had a top speed of about 20 knots, the tugs could only pull us along at about two knots, so it took us two-and-a-half days to reach the Philippines. Nonetheless, we all continued to have a great time. It was an adventure!

When we reached Manila, there were crowds of people, newspaper reporters and photographers on the dock. Cunard put everyone up in three magnificent hotels and told us to call our families – all at no charge. I called every one of our children to tell them we were okay. I think my bill when we checked out was around $1,200, which was paid by Cunard.

The World Cruisers were offered three options. We could fly home immediately. We could continue the World Cruise on the Queen Elizabeth 2, which was just a four-hour flight away. Or we could fly to Japan and continue our World Cruise on the Royal

Viking Sun, which had just been refurbished. We chose the second option because we would arrive home as originally scheduled, rather than two weeks later on the Royal Viking Sun. Even though those additional days would be free, we'd had enough excitement and didn't need another two weeks.

That would prove to be a very smart choice.

So Mason and I, along with many other guests, boarded a chartered flight and joined the QE2 in Singapore. The rest of the cruise was comparatively uneventful, and we had a wonderful time.

The day we arrived back home in Ft. Lauderdale, there was a news broadcast that the Royal Viking Sun – the ship we could have still been on – had hit a reef near Egypt and may be sinking. One hundred and twenty of the same people who had survived a fire were now in danger of sinking! We could have been there! And if I were ever offered a choice between a fire and sinking, I'd choose the fire. What's more, the ship had hit the reef at night, so you can imagine how scary that must have been. (Fortunately, it did not sink and was eventually towed safely to Egypt.)

As you can imagine, a lot of our friends and family thought we would never cruise again after this experience. One of my girlfriends said to me, "It's such a shame that you love cruising so much and you'll never be cruising again." I said to her, "Where is that written?"

Mason and I felt the same way. We were never frightened and, with all the unexpected adventure, we had an even more memorable time. The day after we got home, I received a dozen roses from Cunard. A week later, I got a handmade crystal Waterford ice bucket. And a month later, I got a refund for half of the World Cruise! Cunard was extremely fair, and I'd be willing to bet no one sued over this. In fact, a couple of weeks later, Mason and I were back cruising again.

As for the Sagafjord, she was sold to Saga Shipping a year later, refurbished, and became the Saga Rose. I saw her once after that, but she's permanently retired now. The Royal Viking Sun was refurbished and ultimately sold to Holland America, where she is now called the Prinsendam. Later, I lived fulltime on her for three years.

This experience taught me to never get overly excited when something goes wrong on a ship. There are people smarter than you who are trained to handle any situation. Have faith in them – even when it comes to regularly changing those bathroom light bulbs.

Chapter 2

PIRATES!

Long before the movie *Captain Phillips* with Tom Hanks came out, I had a pirate adventure of my own.

In 2008, I was living fulltime aboard Holland America's Prinsendam, and we were sailing down the east coast of Africa. This meant we would be passing right through the waters frequented by the same Somali pirates who would later be made famous by that film. Although these pirates usually targeted fishing vessels and cargo ships, they had attacked the cruise ship Seabourn Spirit, with 210 passengers, in late 2005. Fortunately, the crew managed to drive off their two speedboats and avoid fire from machine guns and rocket-propelled grenades.

Many people are surprised to learn that piracy at sea did not disappear with Blackbeard. It is still alive and well, especially in certain parts of the world. While Somalia has gotten the most attention, pirates are also still active around the many islands and atolls of Indonesia. Rumor has it there are even some pirate islands there, just like in days of yore. In fact, when Mason and I were on our first World Cruise, and our ship caught fire in the South China Sea, we were smack dab in the middle of pirate country. Although the captain and crew never acknowledged the threat, it was a genuine concern as we drifted without power for days.

Like most people, I didn't know anything about pirates when I started cruising and didn't even think they existed anymore. But I've learned a lot over the years. When a cruise ship is in pirate waters, special lecturers are often brought aboard to discuss the subject because people are always very curious about it. While the Somalis still operate like the pirates of old, chasing down ships and clambering up the sides, others are much more sophisticated. One lecturer told the story of a pirate gang that stole an empty container ship, renamed and repainted it, then sailed into some Asian port. Posing as well-dressed businessmen, the pirates visited various companies, offering to transport their goods overseas. Once they secured a few deals, they loaded the ship and set sail. Of course, they never delivered the cargo to the promised destination. They just took off with it.

When you consider all the money, jewelry and other valuables on board cruise ships, they are no doubt high on ever pirate's wish list. Although cruise ships claim they don't carry any weapons, I really don't know if I can believe that. They must have some way of defending themselves. I do know there is such a thing as a Sound Cannon, or Long-Range Acoustic Device (LRAD). It's a sonic weapon that "shoots" pain-inducing tones over long distances. The Seabourn Spirit reportedly used one to deter its pirate attack, along with high-pressure water hoses. I've never seen a Sound Cannon used, but I know they had one on the Prinsendam.

As we approached Somalia, the ship was on high alert. Extra security men had been brought on earlier in the cruise and stationed around the deck with binoculars. Barbed wire was even strung along the ship's railing, so no one could climb on board. We would be passing through the most dangerous section of sea at night, so in addition to moving at top speed (22 knots), many outside lights were extinguished, and we were told to close our drapes once the sun set. The captain made all these announcements, and he was very serious about it. He also sent the following letter to all the passengers:

2008 Grand Africa Voyage
IMPORTANT NOTICE
April 30, 2008

Ms. Leona Wachtstetter
Stateroom 433

Over the next few days we will be transiting waters where there have been reported piracy incidents. In most of the incidents, which involved small cargo vessels, the ships took avoiding action and prevented any contact with the small, fast launches used by the Somali pirates.

Since our prime concern at Holland America Line is the safety of our passengers and crew, we will be taking additional security measures while the vessel is at sea. We will be running at full speed during our passage and remaining well away from Somali waters. In addition the lights on promenade deck 7 will remain off at night. There will be additional lighting below this level, which will light up the surface of the sea, and a security patrol will be in operation around this deck. The lights on decks 8 and 9 aft will also remain off.

You are therefore requested not to go out on these decks after sunset, as you may not be able to see clearly where you are going. If you wish to walk out on deck at night, please use either deck 11 or 12, which will be lighted as normal.

As a further precautionary measure I may need to use our long-range acoustic devices. This will only be done if I believe it is necessary, to deter fast boats from approaching the Prinsendam. Prior to using these devices I will make an announcement on the PA system requesting everyone to remain inside the vessel and away from balconies and windows as the devices can be extremely loud, although of course they will be directed away from the ship.

If you have any further questions, the Chief Officer, or Security Officer, would be more than happy to answer them.

Thank you for understanding.

Regards,
Captain Christopher M. Turner
Master, ms Prinsendam

After sunset, things went on as usual inside the ship – dinner, entertainment, dancing – but outside everyone was on high alert. You would expect the passengers to be scared in a situation like this. But that wasn't the case. It was obvious that the captain and crew had taken every precaution, and it would be virtually impossible for a band of pirates to clamber up the side of this vessel and commandeer it. So instead, the guests were interested and excited, but calm.

For me, it was just another new adventure. I mean, whoever heard of not being allowed outside on the promenade deck or pulling the plug on that merry string of outdoor ship lights? It was exciting flying through the night in dangerous waters. And what could be done anyway if pirates overran the ship? I suppose I would just have locked myself in my room and not let anyone in.

Believe it or not, I actually slept very well that night, never frightened, feeling well protected, and having a lot of trust in the ability of the crew to handle anything that arose.

The next morning I awoke, a prisoner of no one.

Chapter 3

ROUGH SEAS

People going on a cruise always worry about rough seas and getting seasick. I was in the elevator once with this Japanese couple. I asked how they were enjoying the ship so far, and they shook their heads, made wavy motions with their hands, and grabbed their stomachs.

"Too rough, too rough," they said.

"But how can that be?" I asked. "We're still at the dock!"

Some people worry so much about getting seasick that they convince themselves the ship is moving even when it's not.

I've never gotten seasick in all the years I've been at sea. I've never worn a patch or taken a pill or anything. I actually find rough seas fascinating. It's so interesting to watch the waves and how they break, and the power of the ocean. There's always something to see.

Actually, one of the roughest cruises I ever took was my very first one in 1962 with Mason aboard the SS Florida from Miami to

Nassau. It was the first night, and everybody was sick except us. The show was cancelled, and we were the only ones at the bar. The next morning at breakfast I asked our waiter how he was feeling.

"Pretty good," he said. "I sleep in a hammock, and I only fell out three times."

Now you have to keep in mind that this was the early 1960s when cruise ships were generally leftovers from a much earlier era and didn't have stabilizers like they do today. The rough seas you encounter on ships nowadays are nothing like we had back then. The Florida, which could accommodate about 500 passengers, had been around since 1931 and was one of the most no-frills ships sailing out of Miami at the time. In fact, it was scrapped just a few years after we were on it.

Another time Mason and I were on a smaller ship with our daughter, Cathy, sailing around Cape Horn at the tip of South America. This area is known for rough water, and we didn't escape it. There was an afternoon piano concert scheduled in one of the lounges. The guests filed in and took their seats, and soon this beautiful young woman walked out on stage looking very elegant in a stunning dress. A hush fell over the theater, but as she went to pull the piano bench underneath her to sit down, the ship lurched and she went ass-over-teakettle. You could see her underwear! But I have to give her credit. She stood up as if nothing had happened, smoothed her gown, and said very calmly: "That will be the end of my concert today." Then she took a bow and walked off stage. There might have even been a smattering of applause. Actually, she was lucky. On this cruise in another venue, a piano rolled right off the stage and shattered on the floor. Fortunately, no one was hurt.

I'm really surprised I've never gotten seasick because when I was a little girl I got carsick all the time. Once my father was driving, and he stopped to pick up a police officer walking to work. He got into the back seat with me, which turned out to be a big mistake. I was maybe 10 years old at the time, and I threw up all over this policeman's uniform. He probably thought twice about climbing into the back seat with a kid after that.

I think what prevented me from ever getting seasick was sailing on my father's yacht when I was little. My dad was a very successful dental surgeon, Dr. Joseph W. Davis, and he owned a 36-foot cabin cruiser that slept six. We lived in Freeport, on the South Shore of Long Island, New York, and sailed frequently to Jones Beach. Mom and Dad did lots of entertaining aboard ship on the weekends, so I spent quite a bit of time on the water when I was young.

I remember one time – I must have been 16 or 17 – when I was knitting in the cockpit of the boat. My father and mother were at the wheel, and I decided to sunbathe on the bow. To get there I had to walk along a catwalk. I had the sweater I was knitting and a ball of yarn in one hand, and I was holding onto the top of the cabin with the other. I lost my balance and toppled over while the boat was going full speed. My mother said, "Joe, I think that was Lee that just flew by." I hit the water and all I could think was to dive down to avoid the propellers. I actually heard them overhead. I came up treading water still holding onto that damn sweater with the boat about a mile away. They had to turn around and come back for me. I was very lucky.

On the Crystal Serenity, where I've lived since 2008, my stateroom is on Deck 7 towards the middle of the ship. Even when it's rocky, there's very little movement compared to higher up at the bow and stern. In 2014 as we were sailing from Spain to Monte Carlo in the Mediterranean, the ship got hit by a rogue wave. Just as the name suggests, a rogue wave is unpredictable. The weather might be fine and the seas smooth, but wind, currents and underwater seismic activity can sometimes trigger a giant wave. Fortunately, this one hit at 1:30 a.m. when everybody was sleeping. It shattered three windows in the main dining room, broke a bunch of dishes, and some water came in. The ship supposedly listed pretty significantly when the wave hit, but I slept right through it. I didn't find out what happened until well into the following morning. And the crew had everything cleaned up and the dining room open later that day.

Probably the worst seas I ever encountered were off the coast of Alaska in 1986. It was a cruise organized around the viewing of Halley's Comet. Unfortunately, the wind was ripping at something like 72 mph, and we were flying up in the air and dipping back down for days. Another cruise ship was following us and when we finally reached land, it docked right behind us. We were chatting with some of the passengers from that vessel, and they said, "We're really glad we weren't on your ship, because it looked like you were nose-diving underwater."

Mason and I had a cabin on that cruise where our beds were positioned at right angles to each other. There was a little table in the corner between the heads of each bed. There was a silver water pitcher on this table, and it kept sliding off and getting Mason wet. After this happened three times I finally said, "Let's just put it on the floor." Our daughter was in an adjacent room, and she had some cans of Coke on a shelf. At one point, she had to curl up in a ball because with each nose-dive of the ship, one or two got launched at her.

Me? No bother. I like a little action.

Chapter 4

MEETING THE LOVE OF MY LIFE

Before I get too carried away telling stories about my life at sea, let me tell you a little about my life on land. It'll help you understand where I got my wanderlust and why I decided to sell practically everything I own to live fulltime on a cruise ship.

After finishing my junior year of high school in Freeport, on the South Shore of Long Island, New York, I had nothing to do so -- believe it or not -- I signed up for summer school. Some of my friends had enrolled, and I thought it would be fun. Well, I passed all the courses, and this gave me enough credits to graduate from high school early. I wasn't an outstanding student, just an above-average one, and my mother pushed me to start college. So I went from being really excited about my senior year to suddenly feeling cheated. I missed my prom and Graduation Day with all my friends.

Instead, I enrolled in the pre-nursing program at Adelphi College (now Adelphi University) on Long Island. Despite being a year younger than most of the other freshmen, I didn't feel out of place. I was excited to be on that career track. I had always wanted to be a nurse. The occupation fascinated me, and I liked the challenge of helping people get better. Since my father was a dental surgeon, I had been around medical professionals my whole life. But I had decided early on that I never wanted to be a doctor or marry one. They never got to stay for the whole party; they'd get an emergency call and always have to run.

Along about this time, my father had eye surgery, and the outcome was not positive. In fact, at age 43, he had to give up his successful career. He retired and moved to Hollywood, Florida, with my mother (Agnes) and little brother (Richard). I stayed behind at Adelphi, but a few months after they moved I got a call from my father. "I don't care what you're doing or what you want to be," he said, "you can do it down here. Mom misses you, and we want you to come live with us."

This was the spring of 1946, right after the end of World War II. Easter break was coming up at school, so I decided to go down to Hollywood for two weeks and check it out. Well, probably not five minutes after walking into my parents' house, my mom said, "I'm so glad to see you and, by the way, I have a date for you tomorrow."

"Mom," I replied, "you know I don't do blind dates."

"I know, I know," she said, "but he's the most eligible bachelor in Hollywood, and his father owns the dairy in town."

I insisted I wasn't interested, but she went on to explain how his father delivered the milk in the neighborhood and because our house was the last one on his route, he often stopped for coffee and a chat. Recently, he confessed he had a problem. He and his wife were divorcing. He had asked his boy, Mason, to come home from college because he needed his help with the dairy work and taking care of his Mom and two sisters. They needed a man around the house. But Mason had been in the Marines for a few years and then at college. Everyone he grew up with in town had moved away. His father was worried he would no longer like living here.

That's when Mom volunteered me: "My daughter is coming to visit tomorrow," she told him, "and she doesn't know anybody either."

They had agreed Mason would pick me up at the house the next day at 10 a.m. and, no doubt, enthusiastically congratulated each other on this genius bit of matchmaking.

I was having none of it, though. The next day, I asked my little brother if he wanted to go to the beach at 9:45 a.m. He jumped at the chance and away we went. My mother was not happy. I have to admit, though, I spent all day wondering what my mother said to the "most eligible bachelor in Hollywood" when he showed up and I wasn't there. When I got back home, I casually asked her what happened.

"I didn't say anything," she replied, just as casually, "because he never showed up."

Never showed up? Wait a minute. So you mean he *stood me up?* I was angry. Who did this guy think he was? I suddenly disliked him intensely.

But I did like Hollywood. The weather was great and, to be honest, I missed my family. So I finished the spring semester at Adelphi and then transferred to Jackson Memorial Hospital School of Nursing in Miami, which was just 20 miles from Hollywood. I lived at school during the week and usually spent weekends with my family. I told the blind-date story to my girlfriends, and they all laughed at the guy who had the nerve to stand me up when I wasn't even there.

One weekend afternoon about nine months after all this happened, I was on the beach in Hollywood with my roommate Evelyn. She'd heard me tell this story many times and actually knew who this Mason guy was. I still hadn't met him or spoken to him. By chance, he was playing tennis on the court nearby.

"That's him," said Evelyn.

"Who?" I asked.

"Mason, the one who stood you up," she replied, pointing.

I couldn't believe it. He was gorgeous – very handsome, with a full head of light-colored wavy hair, and he wasn't wearing much of anything – just gym trunks. He looked wonderful. Evelyn and I were both on our stomachs facing the court. After probably spending a long time staring, I turned to her and started chatting, no doubt about how good-looking he was and how I couldn't believe I'd finally seen him. All of a sudden Evelyn got this look on her face and stared over my shoulder. I turned around, and there he was, with two feet planted in the sand, looking like a Goliath looming over us. He had spotted us looking at him and had walked over to introduce himself. He was very pleasant and not stuck up at all. We invited him to sit on our blanket, but he asked if we'd like a cold drink instead. We said "Sure," and he went off to fetch them. As soon as he left, Evelyn stood up.

"What are you doing?" I asked.

"Going for a swim."

"What? I need you to stay here. He's coming back with drinks for us."

"Trust me," she said. "If I'm not here, he'll be more likely to ask you out."

"You're crazy," I told her, but off she went.

Mason soon returned with three drinks, asked where Evelyn had gone, and then immediately sat down on the blanket with me. We chatted for a while and, sure enough, he asked me how often I came home from school. I said most weekends, and he asked if I'd like to go out the following Saturday at 7 o'clock. Of course I said yes.

When Evelyn and I returned to my parents' house later that day, she said to my mom, "Guess who Lee met today? Mason! They have a date for next Saturday. Wouldn't it be funny if they fell in love and married?"

"Well, it's about time," Mom said. "It only took her a year."

When next weekend rolled around, my mother was more excited than I was. I would have been excited, too, had it not been for another encounter I had on the beach shortly after Mason asked me out. A girl I didn't know came up to me and said, "I hear you're going out with Mason on Saturday." I replied that I was, and she warned me I wouldn't like it.

"Whatever time he said he'd pick you up, he'll be late," she told me. "He comes when he's ready. And he won't dress up. He'll come in his work clothes. And if he takes you to the movies, he won't put his arm around you, and afterward he won't take you dancing or for anything to eat, nor will he kiss you goodnight."

And with that, she left.

I didn't know what to think; I was worried I'd made a mistake. Maybe he would stand me up again. I didn't mention anything to my mother, but as 7 o'clock approached on Saturday I was dragging my feet. I didn't want to be all dressed up and waiting when he arrived late in his delivery clothes. But just as the clock was striking seven, the doorbell rang and there was Mason in a suit and tie with a white shirt, looking gorgeous. We went to a movie, and he put his arm around me. Then he took me dancing at the Radio Club and kissed me goodnight. All five things she said wouldn't happen happened!

And while we were dancing, I asked him why he never showed up for our blind date the previous year.

"I don't do blind dates," he said with a smile.

So all my worry was unnecessary. Turns out the girl who told me all that was the town tramp. Mason had dated her, but because of her reputation he never took her places where people might get the wrong impression and start gossiping. Back in those days, Hollywood was a pretty small town.

Mason and I dated regularly after that. At the nursing school where I lived, we had a strict housemother named Mrs. Lynch. She must have been 85 years old at the time. She stationed herself in the office by the front door, checking in guests, and making sure all us girls met curfew.

As part of our nurse training, we worked in Jackson Memorial Hospital. I was usually on the 7 a.m. to 3 p.m. shift. Mason often drove over from Hollywood to see me. He'd always come early in case my shift ended early. He would sit chatting with Mrs. Lynch for hours. She loved him.

A few years later after we married and had our first child, Cathy, we were driving near the nursing school and I suggested Mason stop to show Mrs. Lynch our new baby. I went in first, carrying Cathy, and Mrs. Lynch lit up when she saw us. She came running over and whispered in my ear, "Don't tell me, don't tell me, give me a minute to remember your name." But then she looked over my shoulder and saw my husband approaching.

"Mason!" she screamed, and went over and gave him a big hug, forgetting all about the baby and me!

Imagine that. I'd lived there for three years, and she couldn't remember my name. But Mason, she never forgot! He certainly charmed her – and everyone else.

Chapter 5

THE BIG SECRET

Mason and I dated for two years. His parents divorced shortly after he came home from college. So the dairy, which was supposed to be his business some day, got split up and sold off. Mason bought a delivery truck and went to work for another dairy in the area. We saw each other frequently. When I was a senior, my curfew at the nursing school on weekends was midnight, but Mason had sweet-talked Mrs. Lynch so if we had a "flat tire" or would otherwise be late, I never got in trouble. As I said, she just loved Mason.

In December 1948, I was preparing to go to Johns Hopkins University for three months as part of my psychiatric nurse training. Mason's mother was also getting ready to leave on a month-long trip to Europe. One day he said to me, "Look, we have my mom's house for a month, let's get married."

I thought he was crazy. I had eight months to go to receive my RN degree. I had never missed a day of school and, in fact, there was a rule that you couldn't be married and enrolled at the school. In those days, the belief was a woman couldn't do both, and they also didn't want the older girls dropping out.

I told Mason all this, but he said, "If we don't tell anyone, who will know?"

"Everybody will know!" I insisted. "That's just silly. There's no reason to even talk about it. There's no way we could ever pull it off."

But he wouldn't take no for an answer. He kept talking about it, pointing out that I'd be away from the nursing school for three months, so no one would find out. He eventually won me over, and I agreed to marry him.

We eloped on December 27, 1948. That afternoon we had been invited to a friend's wedding. I got dressed up real fancy, and Mason picked me up at my parents' house. My mom was entertaining some of her friends in the living room when I came down the stairs in my cocktail clothes. And when they saw Mason all dressed up, too, one of them remarked, "You two should be the bride and groom!"

Little did she know that was the plan.

We went to our friends' wedding at the church, but after the ceremony ended and everyone got in their cars and turned right to go to the reception, we turned left. Mason had been up all night making his milk deliveries, but he was so excited he wasn't the least bit tired. We drove nearly 400 miles in 12 hours from Hollywood to Folkston, Georgia, which was just across the border. Unlike Florida, Georgia didn't require a three-day notice, blood tests, or witnesses to get married. We crossed the state line in the wee hours of the morning and pulled over under a gas station overhang, exhausted. Mason had been up for a day and a half. He fell asleep in the seat, and I nodded off with my head in his lap. I don't know how much time passed, but he suddenly jerked awake and put his foot on the brake pedal. He thought he was still driving! I started giggling, and he said, "You can laugh all you want, but you'll never know how close we came to hitting that gas station!"

Shortly thereafter we found a Justice of the Peace, woke him up, and he married us in his pajamas with his wife playing the piano in her nightgown. Then we made a U-turn and headed back home because we had another formal event to attend in Miami that night. I was 20 years old, and Mason was 24. In retrospect, I don't know how we did all that driving with so little sleep. But we were young and in love.

When we got back to Hollywood, we first stopped at Mason's place so he could shower and change into his tuxedo. Then we drove to my parents' house so I could get ready. Mason was waiting for me downstairs and having a bite to eat in the kitchen. I was in my bedroom putting on my evening gown and trying to look innocent when my mother came in.

"So where were you?" she asked.

I was idly digging around in a drawer and said flippantly, "At the nursing school, of course."

"No, you weren't."

"What do you mean, I wasn't there?" I said, indignant.

"I know you weren't because I called, and they told me you went home for the weekend."

Somehow mothers always know. She had me dead to rights, so I told her we had left the wedding and eloped in Georgia.

"I knew it! I absolutely knew it!" she screamed, giving me a big hug.

She confessed that the previous night she had asked my father to calculate how long it would take to drive to Folkston and back. Dad was a genius with figures and after studying the map, he concluded there was no way it could be done in the time frame we had.

Although this was all a surprise, I should say it wasn't really a surprise. We had been dating for a couple years, and everyone was always asking us when we were getting married. My mother wanted a big hotel wedding in New York City because that's where all her friends lived. (Never mind my friends!) And Mason's mother was bending his ear about having a big wedding in Hollywood because, of course, that's where their family was. Meanwhile, my father, who was a very practical man, had been telling us for months, "Don't listen to them, elope and I'll give you the money I would have spent on a big wedding. Why should we spend all that money feeding people you will never see again?"

And he was right. Who needs 14 toasters anyway? Dad stood by his promise and gave us several thousand dollars, which was tremendously helpful starting out. However, my parents did end up throwing us a big "engagement" party at their house on January 16. All our friends and family were there, including one of Mason's best buddies, Tommy Wohl. He and Mason had actually done a short cruise together after graduating from high school. (It was a present from their folks.) At the party Tommy said to Mason, "Well, we're both engaged, I'll bet you'll be the first to get married." To which Mason replied, "I'm not a betting man, but I'll take that one!"

It was all so much fun, and we were so happy and in love, but then in early February I had to leave to study at Johns Hopkins for 84 days. That's right, I had stopped counting the time in months and began counting it in days because I already missed Mason so much. I wrote him a letter every single day, and he wrote me one every single day. There was no email back then, and long-distance was still pretty expensive so we never phoned. I kept those letters for many years but then finally decided to get rid of them because they were pretty explicit. I didn't want my children reading that stuff!

To take my mind off things, I threw myself into my studies. The 17 other girls from the nursing school I was with at Johns Hopkins still didn't know I was married. We'd been together for three years, so we knew each other pretty well, and it was hard to keep this secret from them. But I didn't want to risk being kicked out of school when I was so close to graduating. One day I opened a letter from Mason when one of the girls was nearby, and a $10 bill fell out. She stared at the money. She knew the letter was from Mason and asked why he was sending me money when we weren't married.

"Who says we're not married?" I replied, without thinking.

Well, by 5 p.m. that day I think the entire school knew.

I finished my studies at Johns Hopkins one day early, got on a train, and headed home. Mason met me at the station in Hollywood, and we drove to the Florida Keys for a quick getaway before I had to return to school. Turns out that one extra day complicated my life even more. I got pregnant. That was in May, and I wouldn't be graduating until August. So now I not only had to keep the marriage secret from the nursing school staff but also the fact that I was pregnant. And I was sick from Day 1. My girlfriends covered for me, though. If one of the supervisors was looking for Miss Davis, one girl would say, "I just saw her way down at the other end of the hall." Then when the supervisor came back, another girl would tell her, "She just went the other way." Meanwhile, I was in the ladies room behind the nurse's desk throwing up.

As you can imagine, it got increasingly difficult to keep everything secret as the summer progressed. In retrospect, I think the supervisors knew but just chose to look the other way. I remember one day running by Mrs. Lynch and saying, "Hi Mrs. Lynch, what do you know?"

She replied: "Oh, I *know* but I'll never say a word."

I got the hint.

Now keep in mind that I still wasn't living with Mason or seeing very much of him. He was working his dairy route in Hollywood, and I was living at the nursing school trying to finish my studies and keep up my record of perfect attendance. It was a very unusual situation for a newly married couple about to have a baby. The stress must have gotten to me because three weeks before graduation in August, I started to miscarry. I got one of my friends to drive me to the doctor, who was actually a teacher of obstetrics at the nursing school. He grasped my dilemma immediately and suggested I go to a hospital in Hollywood instead of checking into Jackson Memorial. That way, the school's nursing staff wouldn't find out.

To account for my absence, he suggested I tell them my father had an accident while vacationing in North Carolina. That was a flat-ass lie I thought no one would believe, but I had no choice. If they found out, I'd have to throw away three years of my life. So I had Mason's sister call the school, posing as someone from my family, and report that my father was in a coma and I had gone to be with him. The nursing school staff was very concerned and helpful. And the doctor was somehow able to keep my admittance out of the newspaper. (In those days, everyone who was admitted was put in the paper.)

I did end up miscarrying, and I stayed in the hospital for three days. Then I went to Mason's mother's house for the rest of the week. When I returned to school, everyone asked how my father was. I felt so bad lying to everyone, but it worked. I graduated with my RN degree in August.

Immediately afterward, Mason and I got in the car and headed for Silver Springs to enjoy the honeymoon we had waited eight months to have. Halfway there, we stopped at the Teepee Hotel for the night, which naturally was in the shape of a big teepee. The next morning we got up and turned on the light in the room, but it didn't work. It was a pretty cheap place so we thought maybe they hadn't paid the electric bill. What we didn't know was a hurricane was about to hit. Of course, we hadn't been watching any TV or listening to the radio. As we were driving away, rain was pouring down, the wind was buffeting the car, and trees were actually falling down. It was a tremendous storm. Houses along the road were boarded up. But we never considered turning back. We were going on our honeymoon! Fortunately, we made it safely to Silver Springs.

We were finally together, and we could finally start our life.

Chapter 6

RIGHT PLACE, RIGHT TIME

Mason and I rented a duplex in Hollywood. I got a job as a private-duty nurse, which meant I went anywhere they needed me, mostly to Jackson Memorial but also to other area hospitals. I loved nursing and was paid pretty well. I started at $10 per hour and was soon making $16 per hour, which was good money in those days.

Mason sold his delivery route and worked a variety of jobs. For a while, he co-owned a business called Tropical Farm and Home, which sold plants, seeds, lawn equipment and everything else for the home and garden. Then he got into long-distance truck driving. He'd leave at 3 a.m., drive to wherever he had to deliver his cargo and then usually be home in the evening. Everybody thought we didn't see much of each other, but that wasn't the case because we soon had three children to prove it. Cathy was born in 1951, Billy came along in 1953, and Jimmy arrived in 1955. Three kids perfectly spaced. (Our fourth child, Tommy, came along in 1962.)

Meanwhile, Mason's friend Tommy Wohl had started the Home Federal Savings & Loan Association in Hollywood. As the bank's president, he kept saying he'd love to hire Mason but couldn't afford him because he was making so much money driving trucks. Then one day Mason left on a run to Jacksonville, Florida. While crossing a bridge, the truck's engine exploded, sending fragments of metal through the windshield and past his head. Mason somehow managed to keep the truck under control without hitting any other vehicles or wrecking his cargo. He was real lucky. It was a miracle he wasn't killed. But when he called the trucking company to report what happened, it wasn't very sympathetic. Even though he had done nothing wrong, his boss told him if he had to spend the night in a motel the cost would be taken out of his paycheck.

When he got home and told me this story, I couldn't believe it. "What kind of company is this?" I asked. "Why are you working for people like that?" And after he gave it some thought, he agreed with me.

Shortly thereafter, he went to see Tommy about working at Home Federal. They worked out a deal, Mason took some classes, and in 1959 he was hired as the bank's head real-estate appraiser. I was happy to see Mason leave trucking. By this time, I had left nursing to tend to our growing family, and it was nice to have him working regular hours. I needed all the help I could get because the three kids were driving me crazy. I couldn't even get them all cleaned at the same time. I'd wash one and then he'd go out to play and get all dirty while I was washing the second one.

Around this time, on top of everything else, Mason came down with tonsillitis. He was very sick in bed, and one day the doctor came to see him. (Yes, doctors still made house calls in those days.) I knew this doctor (Dr. Blitz) from my days as a private-duty nurse, so after treating Mason we chatted for a while on the patio. He told me he could really use a good nurse and encouraged me to come back to work. He even promised to find me someone to help around the house and watch the kids.

This was very tempting. I still loved nursing, and I didn't like being tied down at home, so I asked Mason if he'd be okay with me going back to work, and he agreed. Dr. Blitz introduced me to Gertrude, an African-American housekeeper who had worked for his family. She turned out to be a marvelous woman who served as our nanny, housekeeper, cook, and boss for 10 years – never missing a day. She treated our children as if they were her own – very caring but also very opinionated. Unfortunately, one of the reasons she had to work so hard was because her husband was an alcoholic. He used to lay on their couch with a hangover and say, "Gertrude, I'm gonna die." To which she'd reply, "Well then go ahead and do it already!"

One day the phone rang, and I picked it up. When I asked who was calling, the man said, "George Washington."

I thought it was someone playing a trick so I hung up.

Turns out, it was Gertrude's father. His real name was George Washington!

With Gertrude watching the kids, I started working for Dr. Blitz, who was an osteopathic surgeon. Osteopathy was a developing field in those days, and Dr. Blitz started his own clinic and eventually had three doctors working for him. I really enjoyed my time there.

(Flash-forward some 60 years. I was on the Crystal Serenity when I got a voicemail on my stateroom telephone from Dr. Blitz's wife, Harriet. She had seen my name on a plaque on Deck 6 com-memorating guests who have done 100 cruises. She was calling to see if I was the same Lee Wachtstetter who had worked for her late husband all those years ago. It was great to catch up with her and relive those times.)

I worked for Dr. Blitz for four years. Meanwhile, Mason was doing very well at the bank and had been promoted to vice-president. One day he came home from work and out of the blue said he wanted me to quit nursing. I was shocked.

"Why should I do that?" I asked. "I really enjoy it."

"I want to start my own real-estate business," he explained, "and I'd like you to be a part of it from Day 1 – to know what I'm buying, how I'm paying for it, what I've invested, and what I'm getting back."

"It sounds like you need a bookkeeper, not a nurse," I replied.

"Precisely," he said. "And I know you will make a very good one."

I didn't know a thing about bookkeeping, but Mason had never led me wrong, so I trusted him. I quit nursing and went to work for our new business, Wachtstetter Management Company. Although we had a happy and comfortable life at the time, Mason saw great opportunity in the South Florida real-estate market. This was the 1960s, and there was a lot of potential in what was then an under-developed and depressed area. So with the money we had saved, we started buying, renting, and selling properties. It was a risky business but Mason was a very astute appraiser and had lots of connections throughout the area. He would find the properties, close the deals, and then hand them over to me to run because he still had his full-time duties at the bank. I learned the business quickly, mainly because I had no choice.

I'll never forget our first rental property. It was a beautiful, picture-perfect little duplex that almost put us out of business before we even started. I was eight-months pregnant at the time with our fourth child, and I went to inspect the place. It was like a dollhouse. A little old lady had owned it, and she was incredibly organized. When I opened the kitchen utensil drawer, there was a sticker inside that read: "Cleaned January 3." Everything was labeled that way — dishes, silverware, linen…. She had devoted her whole life to keeping things in order, and she had no heirs. All we had to do was buy the place from the bank and find a tenant. In fact, while I was there a man came in and asked, "Is this place for rent?"

"It will be as soon as I own it," I told him.

So Mason and I bought it, but in those days the Florida real-estate market was very seasonal. Although I had a prospect or two, the place stood empty for eight months. We didn't have a lot of money back then, and we were depleting our savings. Mason kept telling me, "Be calm, things will turn around."

Sure enough, it got to be the season again and in one month's time we rented out the front and back of the duplex. It was wonderful for a while until one day I got a phone call from the boy who lived in back.

"Are you aware the people in front moved out?" he asked.

They hadn't said anything to me, so I drove over to see what was going on. They weren't just gone; they had taken everything that wasn't bolted down — the appliances, furniture, linen, silverware…. They had stripped the apartment, put everything in a truck, and left the place in shambles. I couldn't believe it; they had seemed like such nice people.

I immediately called the police. The officer who arrived knew Mason. He looked around and shook his head.

"I have bad news for you. Don't even bother going after them," he said.

"Why?" I replied, not believe what I was hearing.

"Because I know you bought this place from the bank and you don't have any receipts or serial numbers for what was stolen. If I catch them and say, "This is not your stove, they'll say 'Prove it' and you won't be able to."

So we were out the entire contents of the apartment, and despite how patient Mason kept telling me to be, so far he had not earned any points taking me out of nursing and putting me in real estate. We were off to a terrible start, and it was an extremely tense time. But the next season things turned around for good. The market got less seasonal, we found better tenants, bought more properties, and pretty soon we were making some good money. We worked very hard, but we were in the right place at the right time, and we eventually accumulated over 50 properties, which I managed all by myself.

And let me tell you it wasn't easy. I could write another book just about being in the real-estate business. At one point, I was the landlord of a 65-unit apartment building. I got a call from the manager one day saying there was a naked man running around.

"Is he a tenant?" I asked.

"Never saw him before," the manager replied, "although when the police came, he told them he was living in one of the apartments."

Turns out, someone had invited him to stay in their place while they were gone, so he was a guest rather than a tenant and I couldn't evict him. A few days later I got another call from the manager.

"He's back running around naked again," he said.

This time I had the police arrest him for indecent exposure. These were the types of things I had to deal with practically on a daily basis.

One day in 1976 Mason came home and told me about a warehouse complex in Davie, just a mile from our house, that his bank had foreclosed on. It consisted of 10 buildings spanning three blocks. The warehouse was divided into private units ranging in size from 5 x 11 feet to 6,500 square feet. The 200 tenants used them mostly for storage.

Mason said this project was an absolutely flawless vehicle that had nothing wrong with it. It was completely finished, full of tenants, and throwing off enough income to support a family. The previous owner had spent all the profits and never made any mortgage payments.

Mason really wanted to buy it, but because he still worked for the bank he couldn't do it. It would be considered a conflict of interest. Mason had been with the bank for 17 years and was not happy there anymore. The examiners were driving him crazy, nit-picking the accounts, and he was becoming increasingly aggravated. Now he was even more frustrated because he saw the opportunity in this warehouse, but couldn't take advantage of it.

So I said, "If you want to buy it, retire from the bank. You don't enjoy working there anymore, and you love a new challenge." It was so obvious to me, but he was skeptical.

"But if I leave the bank I'll have to buy my own car," he said.

"Big deal," I replied. "Buy your own car."

"But if I leave the bank we'll need to get our own health insurance."

"You can do that, too," I said.

And so I convinced him to retire from his job. We sold 47 of our properties, and I used every penny from the sales to buy that warehouse. It was a very smart decision. Mason was instantly happier, and so was I. Instead of supplying tenants with properties where lots of things could break and need fixing, now I was supplying them with four concrete walls and two electrical outlets. It was so much simpler to run.

I was still on the front lines, though. I had to deal with people and collect rent. Mason got up early and tended to any maintenance then I got to the office around noon. One of our tenants was a local motorcycle gang called the Outlaws. They were all killers, and I didn't want to know what was stashed in their unit, but they always paid me promptly in cash. One day I got a phone call from one of the Outlaws and he was high as a kite. He was vulgar, yelling at me about some nonsense.

"I don't have to listen to this," I said. "I don't abuse you, and I don't take any abuse." Then I hung up.

Two minutes later he called back and said, "I've been thinking about what you said and you're right. I apologize."

After that, the whole gang became very protective of me. If they got wind of some tenant giving me a hard time, they showed up. They became my muscle, and I loved them. They made me feel secure, especially after Mason died.

Anyway, that warehouse complex has continued to throw off income every year since we bought it, and my youngest son Tommy now runs it for me. The proceeds are the main reason I can live like a queen out here at sea.

Chapter 7

HOW I GOT HOOKED ON CRUISING

As I mentioned earlier, my first cruise was in 1962 on the SS Florida. It was a big old ship, ready for retirement, and Mason and I paid $39 per person for a three-day round-trip from Miami to the Bahamas. Back then cruising was nowhere near as popular as it is today. The *Miami Herald* used to publish a list of discounted staterooms at the start of each week. You could also go to the ports in Miami or Ft. Lauderdale and book passage right there, even on the day a ship was leaving.

We took that cruise with two other couples, good friends of ours. Everybody was busy raising families and making a living, so this was an exciting getaway for all of us. Since I had never been on a cruise ship before and had only seen them in movies, I was particularly excited. Plus, while all my friends were getting new cars and new washing machines, I kept getting new babies. I'd only ever been away from home one night, when I took my daughter to my brother's wedding in Arizona.

I think Mason sensed I needed a break, and he came home from work one day and said, "Pack your things, we're going on a cruise." I was 34 years old and had recently had Tommy, our fourth child, and that sounded great to me.

But like I said, the ship was very old and when we checked in and found our cabin, it was nothing like what I'd seen in the movies. (Mason kept saying, "That's because the movies make everything look better than it is!") When it came to niceties, things were very limited. For example, I went looking for the bathroom because there wasn't one in our room. It was down the hall and sometimes you had to stand in line quite some time to use it.

And as if that wasn't enough, it was the roughest cruise I would ever be on. There was a high school graduating class on board and every single one got sick. But come to think of it, they might have been doing some drinking, too. Nonetheless, I had a ball. The food, the entertainment, and the company – everything was wonderful, and I was hooked on cruising.

Our next trip was a Christmas cruise six weeks later on a German ship named the Hanseatic. Because we lived so close to the ports of Ft. Lauderdale and Miami, cruising was very convenient for us. Mason got a great deal on these tickets (I think it was 25 percent off the usual fare) from someone he knew through the bank, so we couldn't turn it down. Fortunately, my mother lived nearby and loved taking care of our kids, even on a moment's notice. They all came down to the dock to see us off, as the stevedores collected our luggage. Even though it was our first Christmas apart as a family, the kids had a great holiday with their Grandma and Grandpa, and we had a great time on the ship. We cruised through the Caribbean and, more than likely, stopped in the Bahamas. (Over the years, I've probably been to the Bahamas 50 times.)

The Hanseatic was the exact opposite of the SS Florida. Although it had first sailed in 1930 (as the Empress of Japan), it had been completely refurbished in 1958. It could accommodate 1,350 passengers, and every cabin had a bathroom. It was the height of luxury in those days. Since it was the holidays, everyone was dressed up every night. The weather was much better, too.

I'll never forget this big German steward who sat at the end of our hall. When you left your room, you had to turn your key over to him. It was a huge key, the kind you get in some European hotels, and he hung it under your cabin number on the wall. So everyone knew where everyone was. But you didn't have to worry about security because, like I said, this was a big German fellow. He ran a tight ship.

I loved being at sea. It was totally different from being at home. No drudgery. I was completely out of my reality. I had finally discovered the type of vacation I enjoyed most. Like I said, I get carsick so I don't like driving trips. Mason and I tried taking the kids into the mountains a few times on car trips, but I'm also afraid of heights so that unnerved me twice as much. But I was made for cruising, and we started doing it more and more.

Most of our early cruises weren't long trips. They were just three-day excursions to the Bahamas or into the Caribbean, weekend trips mostly. Sometimes we would invite friends to join us. Back in those days, the ships welcomed groups and would throw a special cocktail party for you. So we introduced many people to cruising. Some lines even offered special education classes, so I could get the credits I needed to maintain my nursing license while at sea. That was the best of both worlds.

Over the years, Mason and I tried many different cruise lines and ships. We'd study the listings in the *Herald* and book on a Wednesday. I'd pick Mason up at the bank on Friday, we'd cruise all weekend, and then I'd drop him off at the bank on Monday morning. It was cheap and fun. Even travel agents couldn't beat the prices advertised in the *Herald*.

There was only one time we had a bad experience. It was on an old ship called the SS Dolphin. The food and living conditions were horrendous. The dining room was so crowded the waiters struggled to get between the tables. They had to hold their trays of food over their heads. We joked they were carrying trays of steaming garbage. For the first time we didn't eat very much on a cruise.

But like I said that was the exception. As far as I was concerned cruising was the perfect getaway and the ideal vacation.

Chapter 8

MY STINT AS A CAMEL JOCKEY

I enjoy visiting Egypt very much. Those things you hear about all your life – the sphinx, pyramids, and mummies – suddenly you're seeing them firsthand, and it's very exciting. My most memorable trip to Egypt was with Mason, my son Jimmy, and 40 other friends and family members. We all flew there together on a chartered plane to attend a wedding and then took a three-day cruise on the Nile. My son's friend from school was marrying a handsome Egyptian boy. Her family owned a generator company in America, and his family owned a generator company in Egypt. Not only were these two huge companies merging, but their families were also merging. The bride had invited her friends and family and arranged a special group rate. I think we paid $1,100 each for everything. It was a very good deal.

Anyway, the wedding was like a fairy tale. It was in a palace. The bride was blonde and looked like a Barbie doll. The boy was a dark-skinned Egyptian and very good-looking. She arrived at the reception on a camel. There was this little hut on top of the camel, and she was inside it. Her $10,000 dress cascaded down the side. Her entrance was so breathtaking you thought you were at the movies. But as she was being helped out of her camel tepee and everyone was telling her what a magnificent entrance it was, she said, "Don't ever try it. Camels are full of gas, and the gas goes into the tent. I've been choking to death in there!"

One interesting thing about wedding receptions in Egypt is there's no drinking. If you want alcohol, you can bring your own bottle but the host gets charged $50. So out of deference to the host you don't do that. Nonetheless, the wedding festivities went on until 5 a.m. There was show after show, and the festivities seemed to include every known performer in Egypt. It was all really gorgeous.

Afterward, everyone went on the Nile River cruise, including the wedding couple. At some point along the way during one of our many stops, my family came running up to me. "Mom! There's a camel folded up on the ground over there [meaning he was kneeling, as camels do when they're resting]. Go over, back up to him, and sit in the saddle while we take your picture!"

I told them in no uncertain terms I didn't want to ride a camel. But they kept insisting I didn't have to ride it, just sit on it while they took a few quick shots. So I backed up, sat down sidesaddle, and suddenly the camel stood up and became seven feet tall!

I couldn't find the reins and had nothing to hold onto. And away we went! The trainer was running after us at full speed, yelling in camel talk. I never yelled so loud in my life. I was scared to death. I think we ran for a week and a half. Finally, the camel driver caught up to us and grabbed the reins. Otherwise we'd probably still be running.

I will never ever get near another camel again. To me, "camel" is a dirty word.

Chapter 9

LOSING THE LOVE OF MY LIFE

Mason and I celebrated many special occasions while cruising – birthdays, anniversaries – sometimes with the kids, sometimes without. But one trip I'll never forget was in 1997. Mason had always wanted to go on a river cruise, so we booked one along the Mississippi on one of those big paddle wheelers. Unfortunately, Mason didn't feel well the whole time and only made it to dinner a few nights. He kept saying, "I don't know what's wrong with me," but I started to suspect it was something serious. Sure enough, when he went to the doctor after returning home, he was diagnosed with colon cancer.

Mason was a very kind, considerate, thoughtful man with a tremendous sense of humor, but he was also very brave. He was in the Marine Corps for three years during World War II, and his job was to train war dogs. From working in his father's dairy business, he had experience with animals. These dogs were just like Marines. The

Japanese fought from caves on islands in the Pacific, and he trained these dogs to go in after them. If you sent a man into a cave filled with the enemy they would kill him, but a dog would have a better chance of dragging them out. A trainer lives with his dog 24 hours a day – he eats with it, sleeps with it, basically spends every minute of every day with it. The dog depends on the trainer for survival and vice versa.

Mason was in a foxhole situation; I think in Guam. (He never talked much about what happened during the war.) He went to sleep alone with his German Shepherd beside him and a very thick leather leash across his chest. During the night a Japanese sniper climbed a tree overlooking the foxhole and shot at him. The bullet went into the leash at a 45-degree angle and lodged there. I don't know what happened next – Mason never said if he ever killed anyone – but he brought that leash home with the bullet still in it.

Mason always had a soft spot in his heart for dogs after that. We had dozens of them over the years. When he was diagnosed with colon cancer, we had an Akita who just adored him. Because the cancer was so advanced, Mason's health deteriorated pretty quickly. For much of the time, he sat in a recliner in our living room with this dog curled up with his chin on his shoe. For nine months he did that – such a devoted dog.

Although it was very difficult to get Mason to talk about his time in the military, he never gave up being a Marine. About a month before he died, I heard him talking on the phone about a Marine reunion coming up in Chicago. Seventeen of the men he had fought with (now all in their 70s) were going to be there. He ended the conversation by saying, "If I'm still breathing I'll be there."

That seemed ridiculous to me. The poor man could barely move let alone fly to Chicago. But he kept asking me, "Did you get the tickets yet?" Before I attempted a trip like that I thought I better talk to his doctor. So I put him in a wheelchair and took him to the office without an appointment. The doctor said, "What are you doing here?" and I told him he needed to tell Mason why he couldn't go to Chicago for the reunion. But instead the doctor said, "I can promise you he will make it to Chicago, but I can't promise you he will make it back home."

Well, thank you very much, I thought. I'm so glad I brought him here! Now there was no way I could keep Mason from going. He was excited, but in my mind it was a death wish.

Fortunately, our son Jimmy and daughter Cathy and one of my girlfriends agreed to go with us. When we got on the plane and the stewardess saw how frail Mason was, she told us not to worry. She made the pilot aware of the situation and told us if there were any problems, he would radio ahead for paramedics to meet us. I told her that wouldn't be necessary because we weren't flying to Chicago to go to the hospital; we were going to a reunion.

After we landed and everyone got off the plane, we wheeled Mason to a limo, which took us to our hotel. Mason was too weak to get out of bed the entire time, but all 17 of his friends – one by one – came to the room to be with him. It was the most emotional weekend of my life. Jimmy represented him at the reunion and when he came back he told Mason all the stories. Mason insisted on buying breakfast for all his friends the next morning even though he couldn't be there. And when we left the hotel later that day all those guys were out front on the curb waving to him as we drove away.

To my great relief we somehow got him back home, and when I put him to bed I said, "Do you have any idea how many people love you?"

"I'm so lucky," he replied.

That was Mason, always seeing the upside of everything.

Mason died a few days later in hospice. I didn't sleep at all during that time. I thought I was going to collapse from all the strain. But I was so happy I had taken him to Chicago. It meant so much to him and to his friends. He was one tough cookie. He had promised them he'd be there, and he was – a soldier to the end. His friends invited me to the reunion the following year, but I said no thanks. That would have been too emotional.

Mason and I had done 89 cruises together and been all over the world. He was 72 years old and I was 68. The day before he died, he looked at me and said, "Don't you quit cruising."

I wasn't about to argue with him on his deathbed, so I said okay, even though I had never cruised alone before or done much of anything without him. But he always knew what was best for me.

Mason didn't want a funeral so I had him cremated. Afterward, there was a parade of people stopping by and calling the house. The Marines visited, and I gave them the leash that saved his life. It's in a museum now, although I can't remember where. I also got a call from the mayor of the next town over, a woman who was devastated that Mason had died. She told me she had always consulted Mason whenever there was a big government problem and she didn't know how she was going to run the town without him. I didn't even know Mason was helping her. But that was Mason, always helping someone. In fact, he was so admired that the city of Hollywood had invited him to be mayor once. He asked me, "What do you think of me being mayor?" I told him if it's okay with his next wife then it's okay with me. (I didn't think he was right for politics.)

One day not long after his death a representative from Davie City Council stopped by. We had moved to Davie years earlier and bought a big home on 10 acres. Because of our real-estate business,

Mason and I attended all the city council meetings, plus Mason did a lot of free appraisal work for the town. This representative expressed his condolences and said the city wanted to do something special to commemorate Mason. He said it would like to plant a tree in his name.

"A tree?" I said. "Don't bother. If that's the most the city can do for this man who saved the city tens of thousands of dollars, don't do anything because to me it's an insult."

Well, he went back to city council and told them what I'd said, and they agreed with me; Mason deserved more. They ended up dedicating a bridge in his name: the Mason Wachtstetter Memorial Bridge. They had a dedication ceremony and our whole family attended. There will be a bronze plaque there forever with his name and accomplishments on it. The grandkids cut the ribbon.

About three weeks after Mason died, I took a cruise with a girl-friend to get away from it all. While I was at sea, Cathy contacted me and said she had to take the dog to the vet. Now this was a very healthy dog that never had any problems, but suddenly it had developed a tumor the size of a tennis ball on its foot. The vet wanted to operate immediately so I said okay. Two weeks later the tumor came back just as big as before. This time the vet wanted to remove the entire foot, but we'd just been through nine months of watching cancer eat up Mason and we didn't want to see this dog, who had been so devoted to him, suffer the same way, so we put him down. It's funny how we're allowed to treat our animals better than our people.

Two months later, Cathy and my two oldest grandchildren (Billy and Ryan) went on a short cruise out of Miami. At midnight, they all went to the stern of the ship and spread Mason's ashes. They told no one on the ship and had their own service. Mason would have been very pleased. Even though he had wanted to be buried at sea, I just couldn't bring myself to be there to watch it. I knew it would be too emotional, so for once I stayed home.

But I'm glad they did it, because over the years it has been such a comfort to me. In fact, maybe that's why I love cruising so much and feel so at home on the ocean. All I have to do whenever I miss Mason is look out at the sea, and he's there with me.

Chapter 10

QUITE A PAIR OF SEA LEGS

Everyone I meet asks me the same question: Why do I live on a cruise ship when I'm financially secure enough to live anywhere in the world? The answer I always give is not that I love to travel and meet new people, although those things are nice, but it's simply because I love to dance. Even at age 89, I usually dance at least a couple of hours every day. (Unless Perry Grant is aboard, but I'll tell you more about him later.)

On the Crystal Serenity, where I've lived since 2008, there's lots of dancing. There are three dance sessions every night – 5:15 to 6 p.m., 7:45 to 8:30 p.m. and 9:30 p.m. to 12:30 a.m. These take place in the Palm Court, a beautiful space surrounded by windows on Deck 12 at the bow of the ship. The earlier sessions usually have some beautiful sunsets. There's always a live band on stage playing a variety of dance tunes. And in addition to all this, there are group dance lessons every sea day, plus special theme nights such as sock hops and Officers' Balls, which usually take place in the Crystal Cove on Deck 5 outside the formal dining room. Crystal also periodically organizes special ballroom dancing cruises, where they bring on big-name bands such as the Glenn Miller Orchestra and the Tommy Dorsey Orchestra. I never miss a minute of those, but they're so popular and the band takes up so much of the floor that the dancing can be like bumper pool.

I've loved dancing all my life. When I was a little girl, I used to dance on the tops of my father's shoes while he held my hands. In junior high, I had a girlfriend whose parents were very generous and hired a dance instructor to come to their house. We'd invite eight kids from school (four couples), and in the evenings the instructor taught us the basic steps. That was my first exposure to real dancing, and I loved it. In addition to the scheduled school dances, which I never missed, my friends and I danced to canned music in the gym nearly every day. Sometimes we'd even skip lunch to dance. And I loved watching professional dancers. It was mesmerizing.

But then I married a man who didn't like to dance. Although Mason took me dancing at the Radio Club in Hollywood, Florida, on our first date, he was just trying to impress me. We never went dancing on a date after that.

After we were married for a while and Mason started working for the bank, we joined a club for professionals in town. These were doctors, lawyers, accountants, and other important people Mason could network with in order to build the bank's appraising business. The club organized a dance once a month, and we always attended. Mason *had* to dance at these, but he never enjoyed it. He treated it as part of his job. He grew up thinking dancing was for sissies so he never had any formal instruction. He did everything wrong because he didn't know the rules. I tried to get him to take lessons, but he didn't want any part of it. When forced to get out on the dance floor, he would put himself in a corner and stay there. I'd say, "Mason, we have to keep moving." But he would refuse, insisting he didn't want to get in anyone's way. "But Mason," I'd say, "by just standing in one spot we *are* in everybody's way!"

When we started cruising, he'd dance with me once each night then head for the table. Sometimes the music hadn't even finished, and he was going to sit down. I did everything I could to convert him, because he really wasn't as bad as he thought, but he wasn't interested. One night the band was playing a cha-cha, and I was trying to get him to dance. He said, "Lee, you know I don't know how to waltz." That's when I said to myself: *If this man doesn't know the difference between a cha-cha and a waltz then he really is a lost cause!* So I stopped pressuring him. If this was his biggest fault, then I could certainly live with that.

Fortunately, there is a unique job on cruise ships that most people who have never cruised before are always surprised to hear about. Single gentlemen are brought aboard to dance with the unaccompanied ladies. These gentlemen, who are called dance hosts or, in Crystal's case, Ambassador Hosts, are usually very accomplished dancers. They are always present at the group lessons and nightly dance sessions. When I started cruising, just about every cruise line employed them, but over the years as the popularity of ballroom dancing has declined, fewer and fewer ships hire them. Keep in mind that these gentlemen are not gigolos, as many people assume, but rather professional dancers who enable women to do something they love. Although they primarily dance with single or unaccompanied women, they will also dance with married or accompanied ladies if their husbands or partners request it.

This was a godsend for Mason. He would take me over to the hosts and say, "Would you mind dancing with my wife, so I don't have to?" Despite that terrible introduction, they would graciously agree, and I would enjoy one dance with each host. Depending on how many passengers were aboard, sometimes there could be 10 or 12 hosts, which made for a pretty active evening. But here's the interesting thing: While it's okay as far as the ship is concerned for hosts to dance with married women, it's not okay with the single women. That's because you're cutting into what they consider *their* dance time. Hosts must fairly apportion their dances between ladies, and believe me these women keep tabs. They can be vicious; they'll sit by the dance floor with a pad and pencil then go to management and say, "He danced with her four times and me only two times." Those are the tricks of the trade, and it can get disgusting. So when I would be dancing with a host, women would be glaring at me because I had a husband. But I didn't care. I was doing what I loved, and Mason enjoyed watching me – no doubt partially because he was off the hook.

So that was our happy compromise through years of cruising. I'd dance as much as I could when at sea on our periodic getaways and then return to a life on land when I rarely, if ever, danced.

Incidentally, you might be wondering if there are dance *hostesses,* or women who dance with unaccompanied men. The answer is yes. Recently, Crystal brought two hostesses aboard for a special Big Band cruise. But they weren't very popular for several reasons. First, most single men don't like to dance. Second, there just aren't that many older men cruising alone. And third, any guy who wants to dance has plenty of women to choose from already, so why bother with hostesses? It's open season on men out here. The lady passengers will dance with anyone. As a result, these hostesses do a lot of sitting around and talking. The ladies don't like them because they're taking up positions that could be filled by male hosts, and we're always short on those. Don't get me wrong; they're good dancers. But in my opinion they're a total waste. I would also never want that job myself.

After Mason died, I was nervous about cruising alone because I had always traveled with someone. So when I decided to start cruising again, I invited my girlfriend, Marianne, to join me. We were like sisters, and we both loved to dance. She couldn't afford to travel, so I paid her way. To get ready, I also took four months of dance lessons – two to three days per week in Ft. Lauderdale. The instructor was very strict; he often had me in tears, but I learned so much.

Marianne and I did 28 cruises together all around the world. We were in the Mediterranean once, dancing with the hosts, when one of them said, "You should have been here last week; Dancers at Sea was aboard." I'd never heard of Dancers at Sea and asked what they did. He explained that it was a tour group based in Atlanta that consisted of avid ballroom dancers from around the world. Depending on how many women signed up for a particular cruise, Dancers at Sea would supply private hosts. If there were 60 women, there could be as many as 20 hosts, because it was always a 3-to-1 ratio.

This sounded like exactly what I was looking for, so I called them up when I got home and spoke to Wendy, the owner of the company. She was a former nurse turned travel agent, and I liked everything she said. She encouraged me to sign up for their next cruise and fly to Puerto Rico, where she promised to meet me. At the time, I was very hungry for dancing because I'd spent the last 50 years not doing very much of it. So this sounded ideal.

I called up Marianne and told her about my conversation. She said, "If you're going to be with a group of people then you won't need me." This surprised me because Marianne was a wonderful dancer and a great traveling companion, but with the safety net of Dancers at Sea I decided to try cruising alone. I didn't think I'd enjoy it as much, but I did. I spent the next three years with Dancers at Sea, booking every single cruise the group was on, which amounted to one trip about every six weeks.

But even that wasn't enough because I was obsessed. I used Wendy, who knew the cruise ship dance scene very well, to book me on trips in between her outings. I was boarding a ship every two weeks and dancing five-and-a-half hours nearly every day.

Over one Fourth of July, I decided to invite Marianne on a cruise again. Wendy checked around and found us a one-week cruise on Regent. I asked Wendy to make sure there would be dance hosts, and her contact at Regent assured her there would be. Well, the first evening on the ship I looked around and didn't see any hosts. I asked a crewmember, and he told me there were none aboard. No hosts meant no dancing because you can't count on finding other male passengers to dance with. I immediately got in touch with Wendy. I'd paid $4,000 for the two of us, and I was very upset. Wendy was also furious. She called Regent and asked to speak with the person in charge of entertainment. She told him I was her best customer, the main office had lied to us, and now she might lose me as a client. The entertainment manager apologized and told Wendy, "I promise you, she will leave the ship happy."

Well, the next night a young man came over to me. He was about 32 years old, and he introduced himself as the cruise director. But he added, "I am also a stage dancer. I don't know partner dancing very well, but if you're willing to teach me, I'm willing to learn." I explained that I was no teacher, but we gave it a shot, and he quickly became an expert. Everybody was jealous of me dancing exclusively with the cruise director.

The next night another young man approached me. Similar story. He said he was a stage dancer and asked if I would teach him ballroom dancing. He learned just as quickly as the cruise director and, suddenly, from having no one to dance with I had two private hosts. I was the Queen of the May! But it didn't take long for some of the other women to notice, and they started asking why these gentlemen were dancing with me and not with them. "She is our teacher," they explained, "and we're not allowed to dance with anyone else."

I ended up having a ball! The entertainment manager kept his promise, and I left the ship very happy. But that's not the end of the story.

Regent called Wendy a few days after I disembarked and asked if her client was happy. She said yes, but that I was still a bit miffed they had lied in the first place. Upon hearing that, they offered me a $1,000 credit on a future cruise. When Wendy told me that, I said, "What good is a $1,000 credit when it cost me $4,000 to take the cruise and I won't be going back because they don't regularly have dance hosts?"

I continued traveling with Dancers at Sea. I became friendly with one of their hosts, a gentleman named Dieter. He lived in Palm Beach, not far from my house in Davie. We would fly together to meet the ship whenever we were on the same trip. We got to know each other pretty well, but I was much older and we were just travel companions. He had a girlfriend he'd been with for nine years. In fact, she encouraged me to spend afternoons with him when we were home just to keep him out of circulation. We both loved dancing, and we were quite a pair. But I never had the urge to dance competitively. It's cutthroat, plus it's very expensive. You need thousand-dollar dresses and hundred-dollar hairdos. I never wanted to show off. Social dancing is what makes me happy.

Dieter tried to talk me into starting a dance-host business with him. He said I knew more about dance hosting than anyone he ever met – all the ins and outs of it – and that between us we could have a very successful company selecting and training hosts. There was definitely a need for it – still is, as a matter of fact. For example, some hosts come on not knowing what a rhumba is, and they'll ask me to show them how to do it. I'll be thinking: *How in the world did you ever get this job? It's the easiest dance, just four corners of a square.* On the other hand, a really good dance host will attract a following that can result in substantial revenue for the cruise line. Women will book cruises so they can dance with certain hosts, and some even follow them from ship to ship.

Setting up a program to provide quality dance hosts was a great idea, but it never got off the ground. What the hell did I need with a business? I would have all the headaches and less opportunity to dance.

Chapter 11

DECIDING TO LIVE AT SEA

I had a big, beautiful house in Davie. We were in the middle of 10 acres. You turned in at a gate and drove 300 feet up a driveway past a lake. The house was red brick, two stories, and five bedrooms, with a guesthouse out back that each of the kids took to living in for a while, as they got older. There was a patio, swimming pool, and even a little shop where my father, who lived about 10 miles away, did his woodworking. It was a great property that Mason and I bought from the town's mayor when he decided to build another place down the road.

We had lots of great times in this house, and one of the things I miss most about living there are the terrific bonfires I used to build. That's right. Not many people know this about me, but I used to be a part-time pyromaniac.

Being in the warehouse business, tenants were always leaving stuff behind – old kitchens, dining room sets … you name it. It's expensive to rent a dumpster or take it to the junkyard and pay to dispose of it, so I'd burn it. I loved building fires. I'd send my boys down to the warehouse with the truck and tell them to bring back anything made of wood. Then I'd go into the middle of our property and set it on fire. There was nothing else around so if the ashes blew nothing could catch fire. I built some big ones. Sometimes we even had parties around them.

The only problem was it was illegal, and more than a few times the neighbors saw the smoke and huge flames and called the police, thinking our house was on fire. My son Jimmy started out as a fireman in town. Once he was walking down the street, and the fire truck stopped to pick him up on its way to a call. He hopped on the back and ended up at my house. The last thing he expected was to catch hell from his mother because I didn't want them tearing up the lawn and spraying water on this big load of junk I was trying to get rid of.

My youngest son Tommy was the same way. He was the most law-abiding kid you ever saw. If he saw smoke in the backyard when he was coming home, he'd turn around. When I asked him, "Why did you drive in and out?" he'd say, "Because you're going to get arrested and I don't want to be here when it happens."

But I never did.

One day we got a brand new fire chief in town. As I mentioned, Mason did a lot of volunteer work for Davie, and we attended every city council meeting, but this guy didn't know us from Adam. I had a particularly big fire going that day, and he showed up.

"You know I could have you arrested," he said.

"I don't think so," I replied, "and take that truck off my grass."

We had a bit of a standoff, but it didn't take long for him to realize that Jimmy was my son and the city depended on my husband for many things. Eventually, he got into some financial difficulty and we ended up loaning him some money. After that, he became my best friend, and I burned whatever or whenever I liked.

And he was always very punctual with his payments.

After Mason died, the house felt emptier and emptier to me. The kids would stop by, but they had their own lives. I leased a corner of the property to a high-grade landscape architect named Michael. He grew plants and stored his material and equipment there. I was cruising 11 months of the year at this time, and it was comforting to have him on the property every day in case something happened. If I were in China when a hurricane hit South Florida, I wouldn't have to worry so much. He kept an eye on things.

One day I came home from a cruise and this big truck carrying humongous decorative rocks from North Carolina pulled up in my driveway. Then another one pulled in carrying sod. And then a third big truck pulled up loaded with fertilizer. I was sitting in my living room watching all this, feeling like I was in a washing machine as they drove round and round and round trying to figure out where to dump this stuff. Suddenly, I'd had enough.

With no thought whatsoever, I walked out to Michael and said, "You need this place more than I do. Why don't you buy it?"

"I can't believe you said that," he replied. "I said those exact same words to my partner last night. How much do you want for it?"

"How the hell do I know?" I said. "I've lived here for more than 30 years."

Then off the top of my head I added, "Probably a million dollars."

"I'll take it," he said.

Now I know enough about real estate to know that when someone replies that quickly, the property is probably worth a lot more. You never get an answer like that. No ifs, ands, or buts, he said, "You got a deal."

So next I went to see my son Tommy. He's a real estate appraiser just like Mason. I told him I just sold the ranch. He asked for how much, and I told him a million dollars. He said, "Oh Mom, it's worth three million." But I told him I didn't care. I knew Michael would make good use of it, plus he needed it to grow his business. And I had only paid $85,000 for it.

Tommy kept saying I could back out of the deal because I hadn't signed anything, but I refused. The closing was scheduled for a week later. But when I went to my attorney to finalize the details, he said, "You forgot that seven years ago you deeded the property to your children. It's not your house to sell. If you haven't signed anything you can back out."

I had forgotten all about that! But I told him the place was a headache, a worry, a stress, and I was going to stick to what I said and sell it whether I owned it or not. And you know what? I never heard one complaint from any of my kids. Even though the property was deeded to them, they weren't getting any benefit from it while I was alive and living in it. Now they would split a $100,000 deposit and each receive about $2,000 per month from Michael in mortgage payments. It was found money for them.

But that's not the end of the story. About six years later the real estate market in Florida flopped and Michael wasn't able to make the payments. He defaulted, and the kids got the house back! In fact, they recently sold it for a tidy profit. Not a bad deal after all.

So what's the point of this story? Selling that house ultimately enabled me to live at sea permanently. It freed me. Although my dream was never to live on a cruise ship, I hate flying and packing and unpacking and repacking, and in my three years with Dancers at Sea I was doing a lot of that. I don't remember who suggested it, but someone said I should look into living on board fulltime then I'd never have to pack or fly again. That sounded interesting, so I called Valerie, my travel-agent/sister-in-law, and asked her to look into it for me. I told her my only requirement was that the ship have dance hosts year round. I didn't care about anything else – accommodations, itinerary … like I said I had this burning desire, an obsession almost, to dance and pretty much do nothing else.

This was 2005. At the time, I think Cunard might have had one woman living on the Queen, but other than that I don't think there was anyone else doing it. Holland America invited me to stay as long as I liked on its popular, 740-passenger Prinsendam. Ironically, this was the former Royal Viking Sun, which had hit the reef near Egypt and almost sunk years ago. (Mason and I had almost transferred there after our ship caught fire in the South China Sea.) Nonetheless, I decided the Prinsendam had everything I wanted – namely a revolving group of fulltime dance hosts.

Even though I was 77 years old, it wasn't a difficult decision for me to make. I was in good health, I could afford it, I was already traveling 11 months of the year, and now I no longer had a big house to worry about. I mean, think about it: No more cleaning or fixing things around the house, shopping for groceries, booking trips, packing and unpacking, having flights delayed or cancelled, or all the other hassles of everyday life and travel. This arrangement would allow me to continue doing what I loved without wearing myself out. I could do what I wanted when I wanted and only if I wanted. All while being safe, very well taken care of, and having no responsibilities or worries.

I decided to go for it.

I had accumulated a lot of good stuff during my life. I was a collector and had saved everything. Like most people my age, my house was full of stuff. Because I could drive home at the end of most cruises, I bought all kinds of things. One of the boys would usually pick us up at the port in a truck. Once I brought back a 5-foot mahogany giraffe from Africa. Sometimes driving home we looked like the Beverley Hillbillies.

After I sold the place to Michael, I asked my kids if they wanted any of this stuff, thinking they would love to have it. But they told me, "Mom, we've been stealing from you for the last 25 years without you even realizing it, so we don't want the rest." I was shocked!

Instead they talked me into having an estate sale. I put all the most valuable things on the dining room table. The first woman who came in the door at 6 a.m. picked up this beautiful crystal decanter I had paid $100 for 10 years earlier and said, "This is really beautiful. I love it. I'll give you a buck for it." I couldn't believe it! I told her I'd rather drop it on the floor and have it smash into a thousand pieces. What kind of a nut did she take me for?

After that, I told my daughter Cathy that maybe I wasn't going to be the best salesman. She agreed and encouraged me to book a cruise and let her handle the rest of the sale. So I called my agent and said I needed to get away for the weekend and asked if any ships were leaving immediately. She booked me on a three-day cruise out of Miami and when I returned the whole house was empty. Everything had been sold except my clothes. But what else was I going to do? I couldn't take it all with me.

Rather than being sad about parting with such memories, I found it liberating. I was free, and it felt wonderful. I had email to stay in touch with family and whenever the ship came through Miami or Ft. Lauderdale, which was fairly often, I could visit them.

Everyone supported my decision. It just seemed like the next natural step for me.

Lots of guests on the ship say they admire me and would love to do what I do. But when I ask them, "Why don't you?" all I hear are excuses:

1. *"I have a dog, and I have to wait until he dies."*

2. *"I can't leave the children for that long."*

3. *"My grandchildren need me."*

4. *"I'm afraid of being alone."*

5. *"I'll get bored."*

Well, I have answers for each and every one of those excuses:

1. No dog, no matter how cute, should ever keep you from doing something like this (or anything else for that matter).

2. Your children are probably in their 50s or 60s, for heaven's sake. They'll be glad you're not pestering them all the time.

3. Grandkids are great, but they don't <u>need</u> you.

4. You'll feel way more alone in some retirement home than you'll ever feel on a cruise ship.

5. You'll never, ever, get bored. I guarantee it. In fact, there's so much going on, you'll be exhausted.

I took right to living on the Prinsendam. There were plenty of hosts and lots of dancing. One of the things I liked best was that the captain opened each evening's dance session with me! We'd do the first dance together and then everyone else would follow. It was an honor I enjoyed, and the various captains did it routinely for the next three years. I was very fond of that.

Sometimes there would be an Officers' Ball. All the men looked very handsome and dashing in their uniforms. The women could invite the officers to dance on these special evenings, but some of the officers tried to hide behind a post if they saw you coming. Unfortunately, Officers' Balls don't happen much any more on any cruise line, largely because most officers no longer know how to ballroom dance. Back in those days on Holland America and other lines, it was a requirement. They made their officers take lessons.

I actually was in a dance show on the Prinsendam. It was a showcase of the Argentine Tango, which is a very sensuous dance, with the girl running her foot up and down her partner's leg. I was a very good tango dancer, and I was paired with one of the hosts. He was a wonderful dancer, but a perfectionist. Whatever I did was never good enough for him, and I thought he was going to kill me with all his practicing. We practiced for three months, lessons every day, and as the date of the show approached I was close to a nervous breakdown. The showroom was full the night of the performance, and I went on stage and danced as well as I could. We got a lot of applause, but I realized I didn't want to dance to entertain crowds. I want to dance to entertain myself. That was the first (and last) Mama Lee performance.

Speaking of my nickname, Mama Lee, not long after taking up residence on the Prinsendam, one of the Filipino crewmembers approached me. He asked, "Would you mind if I call you Mama Lee?" He explained that "Mama" is a term of respect and devotion in his culture, plus – he hesitated – "it's a lot easier to pronounce and remember than Mrs. Wachtstetter." I had to admit he was right.

That's a mouthful even for Americans, so I agreed. From that moment on, the nickname took hold like wildfire. All the crew and eventually even the passengers started calling me Mama Lee.

I loved my time on the Prinsendam and would probably still be living there today if they hadn't decided to eliminate fulltime dance hosting in 2008. Hosts would still be hired for special cruises, such as the annual Grand Cruise, but that left most of the year without any at all. When I heard that, I told them I was leaving and asked Valerie to find me another ship. She found the Crystal Serenity, a relatively new ship built in 2003 with a 1,070-passenger capacity. It attracts an elite older crowd and routinely wins accolades as the best cruise ship in the world. But, most important, it has dance hosts year round.

I took advantage of the Prinsendam and Serenity being docked in Venice on the same day to switch ships. Cathy and Jimmy flew over from the States to help me move my eight suitcases. I was glad they did. Jimmy is 6-foot-4, a police officer. I was looking for him when I disembarked, but no one was being allowed into the customs area except passengers. So there I was, an old lady trying to collect my eight suitcases and drag them out of the building. I was alone and nobody was offering to help when all of a sudden this good-looking man in street clothes came over and said, "Let me give you a hand. I'm an undercover officer. Your son spotted me right away and asked if I'd help."

It's always total bedlam on disembarkation day, so I didn't have much time to get emotional about leaving all my friends on the Prinsendam. But it was exciting moving onto a new ship, and Crystal's staff immediately made me feel at home.

And, of course, that evening I was on the dance floor.

Chapter 12

MY OCEAN HOME

My address on the Crystal Serenity is Stateroom 7080 port side. It's one of eight handicapped cabins and is 276 total square feet, which is about 50 square feet larger than comparable rooms on the ship. It's no penthouse, though. The largest penthouse is 1,345 square feet (with verandah) and costs an arm and a leg. It's nice, but it would be foolish for me to spend that much money. I don't need a butler or a Jacuzzi or the extra space; all I do is sleep in my room. As soon as I wake up, I leave and don't come back until late afternoon when it's time to get ready for dinner and dancing. I'm always out doing something around the ship, and that's why I like my cabin. It's centrally located on Deck 7. I walk out my door and there's the library, the computer room, the specialty restaurants (Silk Road and Prego), the outside promenade deck, and the elevators if I want to go anywhere else. It's very convenient. I also have lovely stateroom attendants who clean my cabin every morning and do a turndown service at night.

I've been living in 7080 since 2012. I had to wait four years to get it. When I requested it, the room had been pre-booked well into the future because it's so popular. Crystal kept telling me I had to wait. Then finally after the Serenity went into dry dock, I was returning to the ship and the hotel director came running over and said, "We got it!" And Crystal has promised that for as long as I live on the ship, Stateroom 7080 is mine.

I often give tours of my room because people are so curious about how someone could ever live on a ship. But like I said, I sold all my stuff years ago. Now everything I own is in this room. Over the years I've customized things for convenience and to take advantage of the limited space. For example, I used to keep all my earrings loose in a big box, but I have so many I could never find a matching set. So I was in some jewelry store somewhere and saw a display where all the earrings were hung on a piece of polyester foam inside a picture frame hung on the wall. I came back and told one of the ship's carpenters about it, and he built me one, made to measure. He was very proud of himself. Then he built another one for all my pin-back earrings. He used plastic needlepoint backing instead of foam and even put a little door on it. Now all my earrings —and I have hundreds of them from around the world — are displayed, and I can easily pick out a pair to match any outfit.

But then I had a necklace problem. Same thing; I used to keep them loose in a big box. The ship's librarian had an idea. She attached magnets to strips of Formica and stuck them to the metal wall outside my bathroom door. Then she glued wine corks to the Formica and hung the necklaces on them. It was a great solution until the seas got rough. The ship lurched, the bathroom door swung open, and suddenly I had a hundred necklaces on the floor. She came over, looked around, and said, "Oh, that's nothing." (All the staff is like that; there's never a problem that can't be fixed.) She put little pushpins in the ends of the corks, and the necklaces never slid off again.

I get lots of compliments on the way I match my jewelry to my outfits. With this setup, it's easy to pick out what to wear every morning. On one cruise I had a friend stay with me, and I told her not to bring any jewelry; she could use mine. The most fun for her was accessorizing. Plus, I like having all my jewelry displayed. It makes wonderful, colorful decorations and reminds me of the places I've been.

You could say I am the Queen of Junk Jewelry. But it wasn't always that way. When Mason was working for the bank we had a very active social life, and I needed a lot of expensive jewelry. We were representing the bank, and I needed to look good. I kept all of it in a jewelry cabinet at home in my bedroom. Every piece had its own box, and every box had its own drawer. It was all very organized. When we went to formal functions either at home or on cruises, I was really bedecked.

Then I hired this kid as a maintenance person for our 10-acre property in Davie. I'd known him since he was nine years old, and his father was well known in town and had gone to school with Mason. But the kid had been in jail, and I should have known better. He was a wonderful worker, the best one I ever had, but he was also a clever thief. He started stealing my jewelry one piece at a time. I'd pick up a bracelet box, it would be empty, and I'd think: *Where did I put that?* I thought I was going crazy.

Turns out, he was selling pieces that cost thousands of dollars for 25 bucks and using the money to buy drugs. I was devastated. All my jewelry disappeared. Mason told me to replace it, but you can't replace something your mother gave you that she got at age 16. It was all very meaningful stuff, and I was heartbroken. So right then and there I swore I never wanted another piece of expensive jewelry and that I'd just have a good time with costume jewelry.

As far as my clothes, I have one big closet in my cabin with a sliding door. Of course, that's not enough for all my outfits, so I also have five roll-a-long racks against the other walls. They're like the ones you see in department stores, and they're all full with skirts, blouses, and evening gowns. I thought I had 25 blouses, but I counted them the other day and I have 75! My coats, sweaters and shoes are in the closet. I like bright colors. If you'd look in my closet, you'd think, "What a happy closet!"

Just a couple months ago while I was watching television in my stateroom, I noticed all the wasted space above the TV, so I asked if some shelves could be installed up there. All the shelves and special floor-to-ceiling storage in the room are my inventions, and I think the ship's carpenters enjoy the challenge of helping me customize things. I always tip them for their extra work.

The only appliance in the room is a little refrigerator that the stateroom attendant insists on stocking with soda and water even though I never drink it. To tell you the truth, I don't even know what's in mine. I haven't opened it in probably three months. When I first came on Crystal, I ordered a steak in the dining room that turned out to be so big it hung over the plate. It was so delicious I couldn't stand having the leftovers thrown away, so I asked my waiter to wrap it up. I put it in the fridge and then promptly forgot about it. It wasn't nearly as appealing two weeks later when I remembered it.

The guest laundry room is right down the hall. I do my own laundry or use the ship's dry-cleaning service. I have a small sewing machine in my room that I use for minor repairs. It's called the Lil' Sew & Sew. It was a gift from a friend, and it works very well. I used to sew a lot when my kids were young; I made shirts and also drapes for the sunroom. Friends used to tell Mason, "You're so lucky to have a wife who sews." He'd always reply, "Yeah, but we eat a lot better when she's not sewing."

One thing my cabin doesn't have that surprises many people is a veranda. But I don't want one because I'd never sit out there. I don't like to sit by myself. Besides, if I fell overboard, who would know? I just have one big window that overlooks the promenade deck that wraps all the way around the ship. People are walking by my window all the time, and it's fun to watch them. I can see out, but they can't see in. From outside, the window looks like a big mirror. Women are always primping and putting on lipstick. Once I was sitting on my couch and a six-year-old boy was looking in and waving and laughing. Even though he couldn't see me, he knew somebody had to be inside.

Because Deck 7 is so popular, the cabin next to mine is usually occupied. That means I have neighbors. But the walls are fairly soundproof so I don't hear anything. One time I asked the couple next-door if my keeping the TV on all night bothered them. The lady pointed to her husband and said, "It's fine, he's as deaf as a bat."

There was only one time I had a problem. I came into my room and smelled smoke. It was choking me. I looked all around to see where it might be coming from. Finally, I went outside and turned the corner onto the promenade deck, and there was a big ashtray attached to the wall with a whole circle of smokers around it. The ashtray was right outside my window, and the smoke was seeping into my cabin. I complained to the hotel director and the ashtray was moved. As I said, they take very good care of me.

That's pretty much it for my stateroom. When I decided to live at sea, I threw out most of my photos — three garbage cans full of snapshots. As I was sorting through them, I found myself thinking: *Who is this? Whose house is that?* I couldn't remember! So if they're meaningless to me, why keep them? I do have eight big photo albums I keep in my room with shots from the ship, mostly of me with the dance hosts. I love paging through them. And I do have some special photos displayed on the walls — ones of Mason and my grandchildren, although they're all grown up now. And, of course, some of my great-grandson Mason. He just turned three. I really miss him. And I'm waiting on photos of my two newest great-grandchildren, Nolan and Logan. They're twins.

I also have a photo next to the desk that was taken at the bridge in Davie, where there's a bronze plaque commemorating my husband. It shows the grandkids cutting the ribbon on the day the bridge was dedicated to him. And next to that photo is one of my husband and me in Hawaii. It says, "Choose to Be Happy. Live, Laugh and Love." That's how Mason lived, and that's pretty much how I try to live, too. You can choose to be happy or sad. I choose happy.

To brighten up my room, Crystal regularly sends me fresh flowers. Sometimes I'll have several bouquets. There's a fulltime florist on the ship who makes beautiful special arrangements. Crystal used to send me a pound of candy periodically, but I told them to stop that. Flowers are much nicer and not fattening.

If I wanted to, I could have just about anything delivered to my stateroom. Room service is always available, but I have never ordered it because I don't like to eat alone.

If I ever get sick, the doctor even makes house calls. When I first started exercising with a trainer a few years ago, I had never worked out like that before. He worked the hell out of me, and I spent the next day in bed. My stateroom attendant got worried and called the nurse. She came up and asked if I wanted to see the doctor. Since I don't do doctors, I told her I had just overextended myself and needed some rest. I hadn't eaten anything in about 24 hours because I'd been sleeping, sleeping, sleeping, so the nurse gave me a bottle of bright red Gatorade, opened it, and told me to sip it. Well, as soon as she left I passed out, dead to the world, and woke up hours later. Meanwhile, the bottle had tipped over, and I noticed I was lying in a bright red puddle. I thought I had died! My stateroom attendant had to change the entire bed. Poor girl.

Like I said, everything I own is in this room. People have a hard time grasping that concept, but it makes me feel wonderful. Getting rid of all my stuff was such a freeing experience; I felt a load lift off my shoulders. Downsizing is liberating. I had a big house on 10 acres, but I wouldn't want to be living there now all alone. In fact, I'm beginning to think I have too much stuff in my cabin now. Crystal offered me a penthouse for 12 days when I reached the 100-cruise milestone mark with them, but I didn't take it because it would have been a lot of work moving me there and back. What I have here is efficient and sufficient. The more room you have, the more stuff you buy to fill it.

Chapter 13

A TYPICAL DAY (INCLUDING CELEBRITIES!)

Wherever you live, you have a routine. Mine just happens to be on a ship. When Perry Grant's not aboard (I know, I know, I promise I'll tell you about him soon), I usually get up around 9 or 9:30. I like to sleep with the TV on for company, so I watch a little after waking up. On sea days, the ship's cruise director does a 30-minute "Morning Show." He previews what's in store for the day and often features special guests, usually some of the entertainers or lecturers. Then I get dressed and am usually out the door and up at Tastes on Deck 12 for late-risers' breakfast by 10:30. This is a beautiful space with big windows, so whether we're in port or at sea there's always a nice view.

I love to needlepoint, and usually do it for up to 10 hours a day. I like to sit at a table in the Lido or the Palm Court because the light is good. I needlepoint everything Crystal has available. I give small pieces to the crew and bigger ones to the officers. I did a big lion that I gave to my great-grandson Mason. That one took me three months. Needlepointing is addictive. I wake up thinking about it, and I can't put it down. I have two passions: dancing and needlepointing. (Well, make it three now with Perry.) Sometimes if I get back from dancing late at night and I'm all worked up, I'll start needlepointing. Next thing I know, I'll look up at the clock and it'll be 5 a.m. I lose all track of time.

For the last few years, I've been helping teach the needlepoint class. The girl Crystal assigned to be the needlepoint hostess didn't know anything about needlepoint at first, and she called me one day crying. I asked, "How come you're calling me?" and she said, "Because everybody told me to call you." So I took her under my wing, and she was a wonderful student. She paid attention to every word and now she is an excellent teacher. She does a morning class, and there's also an un-hosted session in the afternoon. I'm often at each one.

On sea days there are complimentary dance classes at 1:30 in the Palm Court. All the Ambassador Hosts, plus the lead stage dancers, are there. I used to go to these, but I don't anymore because I know all the basic steps and prefer to needlepoint instead.

Crystal is known for its enrichment program. There are all sorts of free activities for guests, including golf clinics, knitting, keyboard lessons, yoga, digital filmmaking, computer classes, bridge, chorus, and even memoir writing, where I first got the idea of writing and publishing a book about my life (and met my co-author). I took a few Spanish classes, a jewelry-making course, and I also tried watercolors. I painted three sailboats in the ocean. The instructor framed everyone's paintings and displayed them on a shelf in one of the public areas. When I saw mine I didn't even recognize them. They looked pretty good!

There are also lots of lectures, sometimes three or four a day with experts talking about everything from world affairs to Hollywood to the country we'll be visiting next. These lectures are usually held in the Galaxy Lounge on Deck 6, but they're also televised for 24 hours in everyone's stateroom. That's where I usually watch them.

My favorite lecturer of all time was Dr. Ruth Westheimer. She's a German lady, Jewish, four-foot something, who talks very explicitly about sex. She was so delightful and open; nothing fazed her. She would say, "I have no problem with anything two consenting adults decide to do in the privacy of their own kitchen floor." She was filled with those kinds of remarks.

I was needlepointing up in the Lido one day, and Dr. Ruth came over to me. She said, "I remember seeing you the last time I was on the ship. Have I grown?" Sometimes she would even come to needlepoint. She was very social and spent the whole day going from group to group. Those are the best types of lecturers – ones who don't give their talks and then go hide in their cabins, but ones who are out and about on the ship.

So for most of the day, whether we're at sea or in port, I'll be in one of the public lounges on Deck 12 needlepointing. Friends come sit with me. Strangers sit down, too. I enjoy that, and I'm never alone. There's usually a movie in the Hollywood Theater in the afternoon, and I frequently go to those. Then usually around 4 p.m., I'll head back to my room and get ready for the evening. By 5 p.m., I'm dressed and up in the Palm Court for an hour of dancing. Then I go to 6 o'clock dinner. Although there are lots of dining options, I'm usually at Table 14 in the main dining room. It's a table for eight. I always sit facing the windows, and I've been at this table for nine years. In fact, I'm such a fixture that some passengers will request to be seated at "Mama Lee's Table." I do a big return business!

There are some rules at my table, though. There's no talking about sex, politics, or religion. Those are taboo subjects because I've learned they result in arguments and people getting mad at each other. Believe it or not, there have been fights in the dining room over stuff like that – people actually throwing punches at one another. It's ridiculous. So whenever somebody at my table brings up one of those topics I tell them, "Please don't."

After dinner there's always some type of show. Crystal brings aboard lots of top-notch entertainment. Besides the Crystal Showband, the Crystal Ensemble of singers and dancers, the pianists in the Crystal Cove and Avenue Saloon, and the Crystal Sextet, which plays at all the dance sessions, there are also other professional entertainers coming and going every few days. I've met a lot of famous people over the years. Here are a few that stand out for good (and bad) reasons:

Rita Moreno: I met her first on the Prinsendam, and she was very nice. Her husband died, and she was on Crystal several times. She's very approachable, and I always enjoyed her shows.

Regis Philbin: He was on part of the World Cruise a few years ago, and nobody was thrilled with him. He didn't mix well.

Dorothy Hamill: Every year Crystal organizes the World Cruise Games. A former Olympian usually comes on board for the opening ceremonies and to also award the medals. There are all sorts of competitions, from paddle tennis and swimming and mini-golf to solitaire and

Sudoku and backgammon. It's a big deal, and people take it very seriously. I never participate, though. What do I want with medals at my age? Anyway, Dorothy Hamill was very sweet.

Cathy Rigby: She also came on one year for the World Cruise Games. Just as sweet as Dorothy, with a very high regard for her fans. For her lecture, she came on stage doing cartwheels.

Doris Roberts: She may have played the lovable mother on the TV show *Everybody Loves Raymond*, but she wasn't very lovable when she was on the ship. She went around insulting everyone. She put herself up on a pedestal and was very demeaning.

Wayne Newton: Crystal brought him and his entourage aboard one year during the World Cruise. I heard he had eight people with him and was paid a large amount of money for just two shows. Everyone was excited about having him aboard, especially after he did a Q&A in the Galaxy Lounge. He was so congenial; everybody loved him. I'm no groupie, but I even got a picture taken with him where he's kissing my cheek. But then he took the stage in front of a packed house and from the very first note everyone could tell he had no voice. I kept thinking that he would stop at any moment and announce he had laryngitis or something, but he kept singing. I heard later that even 10 years ago in Vegas, he couldn't sing. He's just living on his reputation.

Gabby Giffords: She's the retired senator from Arizona who was shot in the head during an assassination attempt in 2011. She was aboard with her husband, Mark Kelly, the astronaut who commanded the final flight of the Space Shuttle Endeavour. He was a lecturer. I was sitting in the Palm Court one day, and I got a message that Gabby wanted to meet me. She had heard about the woman who lived on the ship. They brought her up to the Palm Court in her wheelchair, and she was just darling. I do hope she's doing better.

Marvin Hamlisch: As soon as he got on the ship, he asked about me. He said he wanted to meet Mama Lee! Can you believe it? Marvin Hamlisch wanted to meet me. He was very nice, friendly, and down-to-earth. Shame that now he's dead.

Nadia Comaneci, Bart Conner and Edwin Moses: All three of these Olympians were aboard for the 2017 World Cruise Games. We cruised the Amazon River with them. Nadia was the first gymnast to score a perfect 10, and she later married Bart Conner, who is also an Olympic gold-medalist gymnast. They make a very nice couple. And Edwin Moses, who won gold at the Olympics in the hurdles, was also very intelligent and cordial.

Meeting famous people like these is another reason I love living on the ship. The best entertainers and the greatest athletes in the world come to me! And sometimes they even ask to meet me as if I was the celebrity! All I have to do is sit back and enjoy it all, and I don't have to pay extra for any of it. I have the world in a nutshell.

Depending on how I feel after a long day like this, I'll either go to bed after the show or do some more dancing. Sometimes I don't get back to my stateroom until well after midnight.

Chapter 14

HOLIDAYS AT SEA

E very day feels like a holiday on the ship. There are parties and dancing and great food every single day of the year. But the staff and crew still do lots of things on the traditional holidays to make them extra special. Here are a few examples:

Christmas: There are more Christmas cookies than you can believe, and the ship is always beautifully decorated. Every major public space has its own big tree. There's a life-size manger scene outside the Palm Court, and there are many, many holiday characters scattered throughout the ship. Every flat surface has a scene – trains, villages, you name it. The Serenity is usually in the Caribbean for Christmas. I think they store all the decorations at a warehouse in Ft. Lauderdale and bring on a special crew to decorate. It all happens overnight, and there's a different theme every year. Last time they used red cardinals.

There are three floor-to-ceiling trees in the Crystal Cove, and one year Gary Hunter, the cruise director, asked if I'd like to hit the switch that turns on all the lights to officially begin the holiday season. It's always a big deal – there's a band and a party and lots of people. Usually it's the captain who hits the switch, but this time Gary asked me. It's a big honor, and I was very flattered. But then I promptly forgot about it and went for a nap. Next thing I knew the phone was ringing. It was Gary yelling, "Aren't you coming down to turn on the lights? Everyone is waiting!"

I never got dressed so fast in my life.

No Christmas would be complete without a visit from Santa. On Christmas Eve, the children all gather in the Galaxy Lounge or the Palm Court, and he comes in with a big bag of presents. Somebody different plays Santa every year, and all the adults try to figure out who it is. Most times it's the cruise director.

Overall, Christmas Eve and Christmas Day are anticipated and celebrated just like they are anyplace else. Guests exchange gifts and so does the crew. I give gifts to the crew all year long, so I usually don't do anything special. Surprisingly, people buy me gifts. Often passengers leave the ship and because I taught them needlepoint or just was friendly with them, they return with a present or send it with a friend. I get all kinds of stuff, usually handmade things. The Japanese are especially big on gifts. But it doesn't make me miss Christmas at home with my family. After Mason died, nobody wanted to be home for the holidays. I've been at sea for Christmas ever since.

One not-so-great thing about the holidays is the number of kids on board. The ship gets infested with them. At 10 at night there are 10-year-olds running up and down the halls yelling. You hear this thundering. They don't realize that old people are trying to sleep in their rooms. Their parents just turn them loose; they don't care where they go because they can't get lost. And the older they get the more damage they do. I saw a teenager undoing the decorations on the staircase leading down to the Cove, and none of the crew stopped him.

Christmas and summer are very heavy with children. They're everywhere. I especially get annoyed when they're on the dance floor unsupervised. One time a grandfather took his five-year-old out on the dance floor, and she pulled away from him. This is very dangerous because dancers aren't looking at knee level. A couple can trip and fall over a child. I went to the bartender and asked if something could be done, but he said he'd been told not to interfere. I thought that was a disgrace. I said, "Some day you'll wish you had interfered when somebody sues."

Anyway, this five-year-old was running through the crowd so I approached the grandfather and told him she's either going to get hurt or hurt somebody. While I was talking, the little girl came over to listen. She looked directly at me, put both hands next to her head, waggled her fingers, and stuck out her tongue. I couldn't believe it!

I waited for the grandfather to correct her, but he didn't say a thing. If that had been one of mine, I would have knocked her flat on the floor. Finally I said to him, "Well I guess you taught her that, too."

That embarrassed him, and they left. But 10 minutes later, the little girl came back with her 10-year-old brother. No sign of the grandfather. But I was ready for them. I stopped them and said, "The dance floor is not for children."

The boy tried to argue with me. "But she's so disappointed," he said.

But I was having none of it. I wouldn't let them near that dance floor.

New Year's Eve: It's crazy, wild, drunk. The ship is always someplace special in the world. Sometimes we're in Sydney Harbor for the big fireworks display over the Opera House, or in Hong Kong for the laser light show. Once the ship even crossed the International Date Line from west to east so we got to celebrate New Year's Eve twice, one night after the other. The countdown to the New Year is usually done in the Cove where there's a big balloon drop and the crew shoots confetti cannons and everyone toasts with champagne and sings *Auld Lang Syne*. It's always a memorable time with lots of dancing.

Valentine's Day: The crew decorates the Cove with red, pink and white balloons. And there's usually a big balloon heart in front of which you can get your picture taken. I have lots of photos of me with different Ambassador Hosts standing there. There's dancing throughout the day, and everyone tries to wear something red. There's a special sweetheart dinner, but my favorite part is the big display of chocolates outside the dining room. They even have those little candy hearts with the messages on them. You can take as many as you want.

St. Patrick's Day: Very festive. The last few years they've brought on this crazy little fiddler named Ian Cooper, who actually looks like a leprechaun. He hops all around. There's also usually a Celtic Legend show in the Galaxy Lounge with lots of tap dancing. I love that. The biggest party of all, though, is in the Avenue Saloon. It's decorated with green-and-white balloons, and they serve green beer and cocktails made with crème de menthe. I'm not Irish, but I always enjoy it.

Easter: I'll never forget the time Cruise Director Rick Spath wore a giant bunny costume. We were off the coast of West Africa on Bom Bom Island. (I'm not making this up. It's a tiny private island. You can look it up.) There was a big party ashore, and he was pretty warm in that costume. His big ears were flopping all around. Another fun thing is that the crew always has an egg-painting contest. One year they used ostrich eggs, and it's amazing what they did with them. I don't know where they find the time because they're all so busy. The eggs are displayed in the Cove, and guests vote to pick a winner. There's also an egg hunt around the ship, and you don't have to be a kid to participate. Some of the little plastic eggs even have prizes inside. And just like on Valentine's Day, there's another display of chocolates outside the dining room, but this one is even better. There are lots of those gold-wrapped Lindt chocolate bunnies, but you have to get there early because they go pretty quick. Fortunately, the crew always saves me a few.

Thanksgiving: Since there's a big meal every night on the ship, it's hard to make this holiday stand out. Plus, only Americans celebrate it, and the ship caters to people from all over the world. The dining room does have the traditional food you anticipate, though, such as turkey and stuffing and pumpkin pie, but they don't do much special celebrating.

Milestone Dinners: When you accumulate a certain number of cruises on Crystal, you're treated to a special dinner. Sometimes these are in the captain's quarters or in the Vintage Room, a very exclusive place that can only accommodate about a dozen people. These dinners are always very special. The captain, cruise director, hotel director and other special staffers and friends attend. Soon I will reach my 300th milestone. One milestone dinner I'll never forget was held in the captain's quarters. As the evening was winding down, the captain invited me into the living room to watch some television. He picked up the remote control, looked at it for a while then asked if I knew how to work it. I thought that was pretty funny.

He's able to drive this big ship all over the world and keep more than a thousand people safe, but he can't figure out the remote.

Birthdays: My favorite holiday of all is my birthday: May 23. It's celebrated like a national holiday on the ship. I hear from the whole world. Last year, the needlepoint instructor came over and told me she just got a new shipment of patterns – all different – and asked if I'd I like to see them before she showed them to anyone else. I said I'd love to. This was about 10 a.m. so I followed her down the hall. She's walking and walking, and I'm wondering, *Where the hell is she taking me? This isn't where they store the needlepoint patterns.*

Well, we took the elevator up to Deck 11 and walked down the hall toward the front of the ship. She was ahead of me so I couldn't ask where we were going. All of a sudden we arrived at the captain's quarters, just in front of the bridge. The door was wide open, which was strange because it's usually locked tight. She walked right in, I followed her, and there were 12 officers in their dress whites with champagne glasses in their hands. And this was at 10 in the morning! They all started singing *Happy Birthday.* On the table was this huge cake with "Happy Birthday Mama Lee" on it. I was flabbergasted. I wasn't even suspicious. Took me totally by surprise. It was so much fun. We toasted and sang; I lost all track of time. I don't know how long I was in there. Then later that day when I came into the Palm Court for dancing around 5:30, the band started playing *Happy Birthday* again. They even had a special dinner for me in the dining room.

Now you tell me: Does that sound better than Christmas, or what?

Chapter 15

HOW I GOT THIS BODY!

In all these years of living aboard ships, I've only spent one day sick in bed, and that was after exercising too much. This surprises a lot of people because they're always reading about the norovirus or other outbreaks on cruise ships, but I've never had a problem. The Crystal Serenity staff works especially hard keeping things ultra-clean. They're always scrubbing, scrubbing, scrubbing. And I try to think positive. I believe the fear of getting sick often makes you sick.

I was born with a good immune system. When I was working as a nurse, I never took a sick day in nine years, and I even cared for patients with leprosy. I just don't catch things. My children had every disease known to man, but I never caught a thing. When they all had the mumps, I was fine. How could I get sick when I had to take care of everyone? The few times I went to the hospital, they gave me a baby. If they didn't have one for me, I didn't go!

I'll admit I did smoke cigarettes when I was younger. But everyone did back then. In fact, doctors promoted smoking in commercials. While I enjoyed the occasional cigarette, I was never addicted. After Mason and I got back from our first World Cruise, I realized I hadn't smoked in three months because I'd never had the urge. So I decided to quit.

I don't have a doctor that I see regularly, I don't take any prescription medication or vitamins, and I don't get regular checkups or blood tests. Some day it may all drop on my head at once, but in the meantime my motto is, "Seek and ye shall find, so I don't seek!" I've found that 90 percent of health problems take care of themselves.

I did have some bloodwork done about six months ago. When I asked the ship's doctor for the results (because he hadn't mentioned them), he said I had the numbers of a teenager and not to worry about it.

I do occasionally have to get shots for yellow fever and other diseases because certain countries require them. Sometimes you have to go off the ship to get these, but Crystal arranges everything. I needed some type of immunization once when the ship was in Barcelona. They arranged for a cab to the hospital, where a nurse was waiting for me, and then a taxi back.

The ship has a very competent medical center, complete with a doctor and a team of nurses. If I have any problems, I can go see them. Once I woke up and I couldn't talk. I felt fine; I'd just lost my voice. I had 10 minutes to kill while waiting for the dining room to open for breakfast, so I decided to walk over to the medical center and chat with the nurses. Nurses know all the good tricks.

I went in and tried explaining in sign language what was wrong, and they finally said, "Oh, you can't talk! Come in here so the doctor can look at you." I was shaking my head no-no-no, I don't need to

HOW I GOT THIS BODY!

see the doctor, but suddenly he shows up, they tell him I can't talk, and before I know it he's looking in my mouth. He doesn't find any swelling or inflammation and says, "You have laryngitis, try not to talk." That's it. When I got back to my room after breakfast, there was a bill for $175. But I was there under false pretenses!

Dental problems are another issue. Years ago, most ships had a dentist aboard in addition to a doctor, but that isn't the case anymore. A few years ago, I had some tooth trouble. We were cruising the west coast of Africa before crossing the Atlantic, so the ship arranged for me to see a dentist in Walvis Bay, Namibia. The night before my appointment I dreamed they dropped me off outside a chickee hut. There was an X-ray machine inside but nowhere to plug it in, and the dentist was a native with no shirt, a feathered hat, grass skirt and a spear. I woke up all flustered and went to the medical center to cancel my appointment. The nurse reassured me that the dentist I'd be seeing was highly qualified and that people from all over Africa came to see him. She talked me into going. But it wasn't easy getting there.

Namibia is mostly desert; in fact, the world's biggest dune is in Walvis Bay. Yet it rained the day we were there for the first time in like 50 years. Four inches fell in a matter of hours. All the streets were flooded, including the one in front of the dental office. When I finally got in, I was surprised by what I found. The dentist was a good-looking blonde fellow from Germany in a powder-blue dental coat, and his office was competently equipped. There was even electricity for the X-ray machine!

It turned out I needed such extensive work that there wasn't enough time to do it. (The ship was only in port one day.) So after we crossed the Atlantic, I flew to Ft. Lauderdale and had the work done there. Drill, drill, drill; it was an even worse nightmare than the chickee hut. The dentist did two months of work in two weeks, so I could rejoin the ship when it reached Miami. Cost me $22,000. That's been the only time I've had to leave the ship for medical reasons.

My father died at age 69 and my mother at 82. No doubt one of the reasons I've outlived them and am so healthy is because I've stayed active by dancing. I did have arthroscopic knee surgery a while back to fix my meniscus. This was long before I started living on ships. The operation went beautifully and I was getting better and better every day until they sent me for therapy. The therapist told me to put a 20-pound weight on my ankle and lift it 20 times. That sounded ambitious to me, but this was his specialty so I followed instructions and quickly undid most of the gains I'd made. The next day I went in on crutches and he said, "If 20 pounds was too heavy, try lifting 10 pounds 40 times." After that session, I could barely walk. I went back the next day in a wheelchair and told him, "I came to say goodbye; you've done enough."

My knee gradually healed by itself. I'm sure all the dancing helped, but I also believe the body has tremendous healing power. Often the medications people take fix one thing but break down something else. Someone once talked me into taking Centrum Silver. That's a multi-vitamin specially designed for older people. When I ran out of pills after about a year, I didn't buy any more because they didn't make me feel any different.

There's a fully equipped gym on the ship with weights and all kinds of machines, plus two personal trainers. A few years ago, I hired one of them to help me lose a few pounds and get in better shape. I am not an admirer of exercise that doesn't involve dancing, but I realized I should be doing more.

He was a nice young boy from England. He developed a complete exercise plan for me. Some days we'd meet at the pool on Deck 12 for a swimming workout. As I was walking down the steps into the pool, he would be right there helping me. I finally said, "You don't have to hold me if I have a rail to hold onto." To which he replied: "Do you know what Crystal would do to me if you fell into the pool?"

That's the kind of care I get around here, and it makes me feel good. He would even swim or walk next to me as I did my 28 laps.

Other days we'd meet in the gym. I had a routine that included all the leg and arm machines, plus the elliptical and treadmill. He'd stand right beside me all the time. We'd meet three or four times a week for 45 minutes. I had never exercised like that before.

After I recovered from that first workout with him, I trained for four months, first with this fellow and then the trainer who replaced him. But after all that working out, I didn't lose any inches or pounds. Both of them kept saying, "Look how strong you're getting!" But I don't need to be strong. On this ship I don't even have to open my own water bottles. The staff does it for me. So since I wasn't getting the results I wanted — and I really didn't enjoy it — I stopped.

I do worry about getting forgetful, though. I find myself grasping for things sometimes, and remembering names is out of the question. I can't remember anybody's name anymore. My mother was diagnosed with Alzheimer's disease at age 79, and I can't help but think I might get it too. She reached a point where she said things that made me realize she didn't even know who I was. She'd ask where I was raised and I'd say, "Your house."

"Really?" she'd reply, "but I never saw you there."

I'd explain that I didn't look like I do now back then; I was a little girl. Then she'd say, "So you must know Joe."

"Yes, Joe was my father."

It was very hurtful to see her like that. She died at age 82. But she never aged physically; she remained a beautiful woman.

I do different things to exercise my brain. I did crossword puzzles my whole life, but now I do needlepoint. That takes a lot of concentration. Make a wrong stitch and it's four times as hard pulling it out as it was putting it in.

I also took a computer class for four months after Crystal gave all the guests on one World Cruise free iPads. I had no choice; I had to learn to use it. Now I stay in touch with my family and friends via email, and I'm even learning how to work Facebook. In fact, the girls in the beauty salon joke they see me more on Facebook than they do in person.

Physically, I'm pretty much intact. I never broke any bones, don't have any artificial joints, and don't even need a walker to get around. I did have cataract surgery in both eyes about 10 years ago, but that worked out fine. I don't wear glasses, just those dollar readers.

A lot of people are surprised I stay so healthy because many of them come down with colds or coughs on the ship. But that's because they're breathing all that recycled air while flying to get here. That's where all the germs are.

I also know my limitations. Most folks don't want to give into age. I see them going off the ship on their own with their walkers; it's stupid. I have a fear of falling. I even have a recurring dream where I'm lying on the sidewalk in some port and people are stepping over me. They're saying, "I don't know who that is," and they just leave me there. I feel very safe on the ship. If I'm in the pool, the pool-boys are watching me so I don't drown. There's nothing to be afraid of here, and that lack of stress and fear also keeps me healthy.

I really should exercise more, though. A few years back I got very friendly with a girl in the computer room named Jackie. She was so helpful; I love her. Well, Jackie talked me into getting one of those FitBits you wear on your wrist. She ordered one for me. It cost $200. When it arrived I read the directions, put it on, and it told me I should walk 10,000 steps per day. I wore it one day. I walked a total of 1,500 steps. It was a relief to give it back to Jackie. It reminded me of how lazy I am.

Cruisin' in a different way with the family.
That's my father (Joe) in the cap; I'm on the far left.

On the family boat with Dad and my little brother (Rick). I'm sitting in the upper left corner. Perhaps this is where I got my love of cruising.

Mason in his Marine uniform. So handsome!

Mason's father owned a dairy in South Florida. This was his delivery truck.

I was in my early 20s when this photo was taken. So young!

Our engagement party on January 16, 1949. (No one except my parents knew we were already married!)

I threw away all my photos when I decided to live at sea. This is the only one I have left from my wedding day. It was taken in Folkston, Georgia, on the day we eloped.

Mason and I always made a great team – in games, in business, in life.

One of our first cruises together.

I always enjoyed
horsing around.
(Still do, as a
matter of fact.)

Mason and I
(how 'bout them
cowboy outfits?),
plus our four kids
at the ranch.

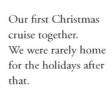

Our first Christmas
cruise together.
We were rarely home
for the holidays after
that.

Mason was happiest when he was with his grandkids.

Just one of the many places Mason and I visited (although I can't recall where we were!)

After Mason died, the town of Davie dedicated a bridge in his honor. The grandkids cut the ribbon.

My late brother, Rick, at my surprise 80th birthday party.

My daughter Cathy became a nurse, just like me.

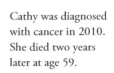

Cathy was diagnosed with cancer in 2010. She died two years later at age 59.

Cathy checked out of hospice to attend my granddaughter Alecia's wedding. This is one of many special moments from that special day.

Mason, my first great-grandchild, was named after my husband.

Alecia's twins, Nolan and Logan, were born 13 weeks premature but they're a handful now.

110

The ship's staff has helped me customize my stateroom. This is the frame they built for holding and displaying my earrings.

I have 160 pairs of earrings from all over the world.
I am the Queen of Junk Jewelry!

This is how I watch the world go by – literally. The view from my stateroom (and, yes, that is an iceberg in the distance).

My roommate, Pumpkin.

On the 2016 Northwest Passage cruise, this Canadian Mountie came on board. He said I passed muster.

From left to right: me, Perry Grant, Marcia and Norma. The girls had these special shirts made up, and we asked Perry to be an honorary posse member.

When Perry is entertaining on board, I'm in the front row
of the Avenue Saloon every night singing along.

So many handsome boyfriends! Just a few of Crystal's many Ambassador
dance hosts, aboard for World Cruise 2017.

Chapter 16

THE MAMA LEE DIET

I struggle with my weight. In the last nine years, I've put on 25 pounds. But I guess that's not so bad when you consider the average person gains one pound per day on a typical cruise. (At that rate, I'd weigh nearly 1¾ tons!)

Let me give you an idea of what I'm up against. Crystal is an all-inclusive ship, which means all the food and beverages (including alcohol) are free. You can order as many courses as you want in any of the restaurants, including the formal dining room, an Italian restaurant called Prego, a Japanese restaurant called Silk Road (that's run by Chef Nobu), and an informal tapas restaurant called Tastes. There's also daily breakfast and lunch buffets, plus afternoon tea, a coffee place, grill, ice cream bar, and let's not forget 24-hour room service. All the food in all these places is fresh and extremely high quality. I don't know how they do it. It seems whenever you sit down anywhere, someone is either giving you a menu or offering a drink.

Guests aboard a typical Crystal cruise consume over 50 pounds of caviar, 4,000 pounds of fresh fish, 30,000 eggs, 600 pounds of fresh strawberries, and well over 4 tons of bananas, oranges, mango, papayas and melons. On the lavish 108-day 2015 Silver Anniversary World Cruise, guests consumed – are you ready for this? – 91,692 cookies, 11,075 pounds of ice cream, 12,200 pounds of beef tenderloin, 4,200 pounds of rack of lamb, 16,420 cans of cola, and 36,450 bottles of wine.

My weight gain came on gradually. I have my own scale on board, and I probably get on it 10 times a day. But because the ship is always moving, you can only get an accurate reading when you're in port. I'm obsessed with my weight because I love to eat and am nervous about what could happen surrounded by all this delicious food.

My biggest temptation is pasta. I'll sit and watch people at my table order pasta and then leave half of it on their plate. I have to really control myself not to ask if I can finish it. Pasta is my weakness.

A typical eating day for me starts with breakfast. Today, for example, I had an omelet with everything, some bacon, half a broiled tomato, tomato juice and decaf coffee. Then I usually have a late lunch in the Lido – a salad with meat, fish or whatever they're serving at the buffet. I'm a good eater. For dinner, if I'm in the dining room, I'll typically order three courses – an appetizer (I love caviar, escargot and oysters), soup, and a half-portion of the entrée. My all-time favorite entrée is roast beef. When I was growing up, my family had a standing rib roast every Sunday. I like my beef rare. My mother used to say, "To cook a steak for Lee just put it on a plate raw, run past the stove, and it will be just right. I also love the Japanese food at Silk Road, especially the sushi.

When it comes to dessert, I try to watch it. I'll have sherbet or something sugar-free. If I even get close to a rich dessert like bananas foster or Grand Marnier soufflé (both specialties in the dining room), the calories jump off and onto me.

I mentioned the ice cream bar. It serves Ben and Jerry's exclusively, all the best flavors, and you can build your own sundaes or milkshakes. I used to be a big ice-cream person, but I try to limit myself to one scoop per day now. My favorite flavor is Americone Dream, which contains little pieces of fudge-covered waffle cone. It's really good.

Next to the ice-cream bar, most people's downfall calorie-wise is the real bar. The ship is all-inclusive so all the alcohol (except for the really expensive stuff) is free. I drink very little, occasionally a glass of white zinfandel or an apple or raspberry martini. Most of the time when I order something it's to be sociable and please somebody else. I really don't like the taste of it. I never in my life finished a whole beer. I used to work at that, because my three boys love beer. They'd buy it by the keg, and I'd try to drink a whole glass, but I never could get one down.

Although I don't drink much alcohol and try to go easy on sweets, there is so much good food on the ship that your weight can get away from you even if you're vigilant. And I really try to be. Since I live on the ship, it's easier not to be taken in by everything I see because I know if I don't order it today or even this week, I can have it tomorrow or next week. When you're only on the ship for a short time, like most passengers, you don't think like that.

The ship does make it easy to eat healthy, if you so choose. Fruits and vegetables are cut up and available at every meal. Portion sizes in the dining room are small, so you can eat in moderation (or like I do, order a half-portion). I've seen people lose up to 20 pounds on a three-month World Cruise. But then again, I've seen people gain 20 pounds and more on a three-month World Cruise. They have this feeling that, "I'm paying all this money, so I'm going to eat everything in sight."

I feel any weight gain first while dancing. That's when I know I need to do something. One of the golf pros on board recommended a juice diet called "Reboot With Joe." I went on that for four months a while back and lost 23 pounds. I drank 16 ounces of fresh-squeezed juice for breakfast, 16 ounces for lunch, 16 ounces for an afternoon snack, and 16 ounces for dinner. After a while, I didn't even need to order them; the kitchen had all the recipes so when the wait staff saw me coming they'd have it on the table before I even sat down.

On the third day of my juice diet I was invited to the captain's quarters for dinner. They always have the best food there, but I knew if I cheated so early in the diet I would be prone to cheat again. So I had my juice delivered to his quarters and just sipped it while everyone else was eating all this gorgeous food. I don't think the captain will ever recover. Everybody else was eating like a king, and I had a glass of juice in front of me.

This was the first time I ever tried an all-liquid diet, and it was hard at first. To help me, the wait staff would joke, "This one has steak in it, this one has ham, this one has some fish…." It wasn't just the sight of all the good food that was tempting but also the smell of it. After a while I went back to eating solid food for dinner. But I stuck with juice for the rest of the day, and it worked out well. I got a lot of compliments on how I looked. The golf pro says she does the juice diet periodically to stay trim. She also says it improves her memory and makes her feel brighter, but I didn't experience any of that.

I'm off the juice diet now, though, and I won't do that again. I melted off 23 pounds, but I missed regular food too much. And unfortunately, I've put all that weight back on.

Nonetheless, this is another great example of why it's so great living on the ship. If I had to go out and shop for all those different fruits and vegetables and then spend the time juicing them myself, I never would have even tried this diet in the first place. It would also have been very expensive because of the special blenders you need. But on the ship they did all that for me.

You know, come to think of it, I can't even remember the last time I cooked or, or for that matter, made myself anything!

Chapter 17

THE BEST (AND WORST)
PLACES I'VE BEEN

I've been fortunate to see just about everything in the world, or at least everything that has a port nearby. I can't tell you how many countries I've visited, but it's a lot. I used to have a map of the world hanging on the wall at home. We'd put a pin in every country we visited. The thing was solid with pins. One day it fell down, hit the floor, and those pins scattered everywhere. I swept them up and put them in the garbage.

I have some favorite places and some cruises I'll never forget, but there are also countries I wouldn't mind never seeing again. Here are a few of the best and worst:

Northwest Passage: This cruise was one of the best I've taken. I loved it, probably because it was something entirely new. In mid-August 2016, the Serenity left Seward, Alaska, went north through the Bering Strait, and then sailed east across the top of Canada all the way to Greenland and eventually down to New York City. We were the largest cruise ship to ever get through the Northwest Passage. It took us 32 days to do what took other ships years, if they succeeded at all. Of course, it's different now. There's a big worry about the ice disappearing. The whole top of the world has melted back. We went for a quite a while without seeing any ice at all. In fact, passengers started complaining: "What did we pay all this money for? Where are the polar bears?" Well, if there's no ice, there are no polar bears.

Fortunately, we had an icebreaker escorting us, the RSS Ernest Shackleton. It had two helicopters on board, and I heard they sent them up to search for polar bears. They found a mother and her cubs adrift on an iceberg, and then later that same afternoon a big male on another iceberg that had just killed a seal. There was blood everywhere.

Seeing polar bears was the most memorable part of the trip for me. Crystal installed a special camera on the front of the ship and two big-screen TVs in the Palm Court so you could sit and watch everything as if you were in a movie theater. Those TVs had the best reception I've ever seen. There was a fulltime cameraman with the job of finding animals and putting them on the big screen.

There were also many lectures by scientists who were very knowledgeable and informative about the Arctic. I watched some of them. One thing I learned: I don't know when the Eskimos stopped calling themselves Eskimos, but I don't like it. I have a hard time remembering and pronouncing Inuits. They sure are a happy people, though – possibly the happiest people in the world. I was fascinated when some of them came aboard. Always smiling, with delightful children. They even sang for us, although their idea of singing (they call it "throat singing") is a bit unusual.

One thing I didn't do is get into those big black rafts. I think they call them Zodiacs. One day I was looking out the window, and the Zodiacs were full of people returning from Beechey Island. It was so windy it was snowing sideways. After this one little Zodiac dropped off all its passengers, it turned around and started going back to shore. The wind pushed its nose up in the air so all the pilot could see was the floor of the raft. That was interesting to watch. And believe me, if one person were to fall overboard, it would be me. The staff and crew took such tremendous care to insure that nobody got hurt. Crystal spent three years preparing for this trip, every detail, and everything was perfect, including the weather.

There was one thing that wasn't perfect, though – those damn red coats. Each guest got a big parka with a fur-lined hood. It took me three tries before I found one that fit. The first one wouldn't zip up. They're made in China, where people are a lot smaller than they are here. So they took it back and brought me another one. I could zip this one up, but I couldn't sit down in it. So they took that one back and brought me a third one. It zipped up, I could sit down, but it wasn't that comfortable. The only time I wore it was when they took a picture of all 800 passengers out on deck after we'd done the Passage. Now it's hanging in my closet, and I'm praying they don't give me another one when we do the Northwest Passage again in 2017. I can't close my closet door anymore.

Antarctica: Five and a half months later, in late February 2017, I was at the other end of the world. I don't think many people can say they've been to the Arctic and Antarctic in less than six months. I'd been to Antarctica a number of times before. From Cape Horn at the tip of South America, you sail across the Drake Passage, which can have some of the roughest seas in the world. Then you cruise along the Antarctic Peninsula over to Elephant Island. We usually spend about a week down there. I don't have a favorite when it comes to picking between the Arctic and the Antarctic. The biggest differences are that one has lots of snow and ice and the other no longer does. And one has lots of penguins and the other has polar bears. They're both exciting, though.

Ushuaia, Argentina: This is the southernmost city in the world, at the very tip of South America. It's a raw place with very changeable weather, but it has its charm. I've been here dozens of times over the years. When I was living on the Prinsendam, I got off the ship and asked a policeman if he knew a place where I could get my nails done. (Believe me, it's a lot cheaper than having them done on the ship.) He said, "Come on, I'll take you there," and just like that he took my hand and walked me all the way to a beauty parlor. He even went inside with me to see if they could squeeze me in. People can be very nice in other countries. Those ladies did a fine job on my nails, too.

African Safari: I've only been on one African safari, but I'll never forget it. Years ago, two dance hosts invited my girlfriend and me on one. The ship was offering an overnight excursion to the famous Treetops Hotel in Aberdare National Park, Kenya. It's an actual treehouse, and the ship's price was $1,200 per person. But one of the hosts had a friend at a local travel agency who got us the same deal for $200 per person. That was too good to pass up, so we hired a private car with a driver and set off.

There was a gate at the entrance to the park where you had to stop and check in. One of the hosts was an exercise nut, a fanatic about running, so since the hotel was only about a mile away he decided to run there. We thought nothing of it, and the guard at the gate didn't notice him get out of the car. When we reached the hotel we were waiting and waiting for him. Finally, a car pulled up and a very upset dance host got out.

"They wanted to put me in jail!" he said.

Rangers had stopped him, asked what he was doing, and said that was the stupidest thing they'd ever seen.

"You're lucky the animals didn't eat you," they told him. "We don't go anywhere without our guns."

So that was a pretty wild beginning to our safari. The next day we got up at 6 a.m. and rode in all-terrain vehicles to see lots of animals. Then we ate at the hotel on a big elevated patio overlooking a waterhole with elephants and lions. We even managed to squeeze in some shopping at a mahogany factory where I bought that five-foot giraffe I mentioned earlier.

It was a great trip. But on the drive back to the ship, on the main road leading into town, we stopped for a red light. There was a six-foot chain-link fence alongside the road about an arm's-length away. As we sat there, I saw this black man running full speed on the other side of the fence with two policemen with rifles chasing him. I'll never forget how big his eyes were. That's how close we were! And I remember thinking, "If that light doesn't change we're going to witness a murder." Fortunately, the light did change and we sped off. I still wonder to this day if they shot him or not.

Crossing the Equator: Whenever the ship does this, there's an Equator Crossing Ceremony. If you've never crossed the equator before you're called a "pollywog" and once you do you become a "shellback". The ceremony is usually held around the pool with King Neptune and His Court officiating. All pollywogs must kiss a huge fish on the mouth in order to become an official shellback and, of course, there's lots of drinking and singing and dancing and more than a few people end up getting tossed into the pool, including the captain and cruise director. Afterward you get a very official-looking Equator Crossing Certificate that reads:

> *Greetings to all ye Mortals on this Good Planet Earth.*
>
> *Be it known to all that I, Neptune Rex, Monarch and Ruler of All the Oceans and the Seven Seas, do hereby proclaim that the former landlubber known as [your name printed here] has, in a relatively sane and sober condition, crossed the line which divides the North from the South on My Watery Dominions, known to all as The Equator.*
>
> *This Subject, having appeared within Our Royal Domain aboard the Good Ship Crystal Serenity has been found to be numbered as one of our trusty shellbacks and is hereby initiated into the Ancient Order of the Solemn Mysteries of the Deep, with all rights and privileges pertaining thereto: To cruise without impediment or hindrance from wind or wave, whirlpool or waterspout, including payment of hush money and contributions to the fishes welcoming all ships passing through My Domain.*
>
> *Given to our newly initiated subject on this date [xxx] by my colleague and trusted friend, the good Captain of this vessel.*
>
> *[Captain's signature]*

As I said the certificates are very nice, but I asked them to please stop sending them to me because I had so many.

China: Mason and I were on one of the first trips to China – a three-day excursion during one of our cruises – just after Nixon opened up the country to Americans. In fact, we rode in the same limo that Nixon used when he was there. We kept seeing big groups of Chinese standing at the edges of places in Beijing as we passed by. I finally asked our guide, "Why are they standing there looking at us?" He said it was because they'd never seen a blonde woman before, and they were hoping to see one in our group. I was happy my hair was almost black so I wouldn't be noticed.

China back then was not like it is today. Bicycles were everywhere, now its all cars. But the traffic was still unbelievable, and so was the pollution. When I first saw Chinese in pictures riding bicycles and wearing surgical masks, I thought: *How very nice and considerate, they have colds and don't want to transfer it.* But it was because the sand from the Gobi Desert and the pollution in Beijing was so bad. The other thing I remember is the rows of beautiful hotels. It almost looked like Collins Avenue in Miami. But when you checked into your room and looked out the back window, there was nothing behind them.

On one of our side-trips we visited the Great Wall, where I took a fall. I was walking, there was a hole in the ground, and I stepped in it. I was standing up then all of a sudden I was lying on the ground. Mason was mortified. He wanted to pull me right up but you never do that to someone who has fallen. You let them stay down to regain their wits and check to see if anything is broken. Fortunately I was okay. The Wall is impressive, but now I think of it as The Fall.

I loved the food in China. We ate in this restaurant at a table with a huge Lazy Susan in the middle with a million things on it, none of which could be identified. I'm an adventurous eater, and I tried everything. After the meal we went outside, and there was a man waiting for his wife. Mason asked him what he thought of the meal, and he said he was disappointed.

"Why are you disappointed?" asked Mason.

"Because I've always wanted to know what Great Dane tasted like, and I think they served us poodle."

When I overheard that I thought: *Oh my God, what have I done?* Suddenly I was afraid I had been eating dog meat. Funny how people say things, and you realize you had never even thought of that possibility.

I've been back to China with Crystal many times since then. Since the nearest port is Tianjin, they usually put everyone on big buses for the two- to three-hour drive into Beijing. Then they put you up in two big hotels. They even rent out the Great Hall of the People on Tiananmen Square and host a dinner with live entertainment. It's always a great evening.

One thing I'm less excited about in China is the plumbing. We made a pit stop with the bus and had to wait in this long line to use the bathroom. When I finally opened the door, there was a hole in the ground.

Russia: While on a bus heading to Saint Petersburg I saw two women walking along the highway in black, ankle-length dresses. I knew they weren't nuns because they had shovels over their shoulders. This was customary here. The women went to work while the men stayed home and drank vodka. It left me not-so fond of the Russians. I grew more impressed, though, when we drove into the city. In front of the bridge were these stanchions with solid gold balls on top. But it didn't make any sense. Amidst such luxury, there were long lines of people trying to buy food. Russia is a very mixed up place.

Iran: The Serenity made a maiden call at the port of Bandar Abbas in 2010. There was lots of controversy leading up to it because of the political situation in Iran at the time. I didn't risk getting off the ship. No way were they taking me hostage.

Rome: It's very crowded. I visited Vatican City and St. Peter's Basilica. I went into the church and sat down in an aisle seat. All of a sudden all these bishops from all over the world came walking down the aisle. It was like a parade, and I just happened to be there. I think it was a bishops' convention, and it was something to see.

Turkey: A lot of my clothes come from Istanbul. They have wonderful things there. There was a dress in the Grand Bazaar that the shopkeeper wanted $200 for. It was a gorgeous, navy blue dress with all kinds of stones down the front and back. But I wasn't about to pay $200 for it, and the owner of the shop wouldn't negotiate. So I walked out, turned the corner, and went into this place no bigger than a closet. And there was the same exact dress folded up in a cellophane bag for $25. I couldn't believe it. I bought it, and I wore that dress so much I actually ended up wearing it out; it was a real showstopper. People always commented that they'd never seen a dress like that before. In fact, I enjoyed that dress so much when we were in Istanbul about 10 years later I went back to the same shop and bought it again – only this time in maroon. Unfortunately, the price had gone up to $100. But I figured between the two of them I'd gotten my money's worth.

Hong Kong: This used to be another one of my favorite shopping cities. For $80 you could fill a laundry basket with costume jewelry. Sometimes I bought so much I could hardly carry it back to the ship. But not anymore, it's all designer stuff and most of the bargains are gone.

Japan: Mason and I got on the subway once and after I sat down I noticed this beautiful red umbrella leaning against the seat. I said, "Look at this; somebody left it for me." Mason was so law-abiding he wanted me to leave it, but I knew if I didn't take it the next person would. I used that umbrella for the next 10 years. It represented

Japan to me. I love Japanese food; I eat everything they make. But in all these years I never mastered chopsticks. When I go to Silk Road on the ship, the waiters always give me "American chopsticks."

India: All my life I said, "I don't ever want to go to India." That's because I'd never heard anything good about it. But Mason wanted to go, so I told him to take Cathy and I'd stay home and run the business. So the two of them went. They sent me a photo of a donkey pulling a mower at the Taj Mahal, which was typical of Mason because he was always mowing at home. They had a ball and told me I'd love it too, so we signed up for a world cruise that stopped there. It was crowded and dirty and poor, just as I expected, but it was also fascinating. All the women dress in these saris made of beautiful material. I had one custom made. It was gorgeous but a royal pain to get in and out of. It was one piece – six yards of material that you wrapped around and around and up and through. When you went to the ladies' room you just couldn't lift it; you had to take the whole thing off. It was a lot of work. I made it into something else.

Guam: Mason and I went to Guam in 1994 for the 50th anniversary of the liberation of the island by American forces. He was there during the war, so it was pretty emotional for him. We were walking down the street and three children stopped us and said, "Our grandfather told us what the Marines did for us, and we want to thank you." It was very touching. I also remember being in a hotel while Mason was sleeping and opening the drapes to see a huge fireworks display going on outside. It was gorgeous. I watched it all alone while he slept through it. To this day, it was the best display I've ever seen, and I've seen a lot of fireworks.

Rio de Janeiro: It's one of the most beautiful sail-ins in the world, as you cruise by Christ the Redeemer statue and Sugarloaf Mountain. Mason and I were in Rio once, driving along famous Copacabana

Beach. There was a woman sitting in a chair and a man putting lotion on her back. They were so close to the road you couldn't miss them. She turned around, and there she was in the altogether, totally naked, right by our taxi! I really thought Mason was going to crawl out of the car.

Alaska: I'm intrigued by the stories about the houses of prostitution they had up there during the Gold Rush. There's actually a place in Ketchikan on Creek Street called Dolly's House Museum. It's a house of ill repute that's been completely restored. There are even actresses dressed as prostitutes outside inviting you in. I find that interesting.

Panama Canal: I've probably been though it about 50 times. I like watching the ship rise up and then drop down about 84 feet through the locks. I never tire of it.

Caribbean: Oh God. I've been all through there hundreds of times. I know every inch of it, just like the back of my hand.

Crystal Serenity: People think I'm adventurous, but I don't want to climb mountains or go off exploring by myself. Far and away, of all the places I've been, this ship is my favorite destination. In fact, I've discovered that when we're in port I can see 90% of what people see without leaving the ship.

Passengers will come back exhausted after exploring some Third World port, see me sitting up on the Lido doing needlepoint, and say, "Boy, did you have the right idea."

But I never encourage anyone to stay on board when we're in port. I love it when everyone goes ashore. Then the whole ship is mine – my private yacht!

Chapter 18

'KIDNAPPED' IN THAILAND

I hardly ever get off the ship any more. Occasionally, I'll go ashore to do a little shopping in a place I enjoy like Kusadasi or Istanbul, but only if someone escorts me. I always try to go to the special shore-side events Crystal organizes during the annual World Cruise because they're so spectacular. In past years, they've thrown parties in Egypt (with a laser light show on the pyramids), Dubai (with a *Lawrence of Arabia* theme), Hobbiton in New Zealand (with exclusive access to the site where *Lord of the Rings* was filmed), and even Pompeii (with an evening concert in the ancient Roman amphitheater). But I never go off the ship by myself anymore, and here's why.

A few years ago, the Serenity was in Phuket, Thailand, for the day, and I wanted to buy some aspirin and also one of those sarongs – the long colorful wraps that Thai women wear. In most ports, Crystal supplies a free shuttle bus into town. Since the bus was supposed to drop us off at a very good hotel in the center of Phuket, I decided to ride it in, get what I needed, and take the bus back.

The hotel was beautiful. I went to the front desk and asked if there was somewhere I could buy aspirin. They told me to walk a block down the street, and I'd find a pharmacy. So I started walking. Well, the "street" was a dirt road, very antiquated and difficult to negotiate. All of a sudden, I got this feeling I was no longer alone and when I looked up there was this little guy walking next to me.

"Welcome to Phuket," he said. "I would like to take you on a tour."

"I'm sure you would," I said and kept walking.

Now in Phuket most people get around in what are called "tuk-tuks." These are three-wheel auto rickshaws. They're called tuk-tuks because that's the sound their little engines make: tuk-tuk-tuk-tuk-tuk. They're the taxi of Southeast Asia. In Phuket, there must be thousands of them; they're everywhere. So this little guy keeps walking next to me, saying he wants to take me on a tour. And I keep telling him I'm not looking to take a tour; I just want to buy some aspirin at the pharmacy, which by this time I could see up ahead.

"I will take you anywhere you want to go for a dollar," he persisted.

"That's very nice," I said, "but all I'm interested in is buying some aspirin and maybe a sarong, and then going right back to the…."

Suddenly, he grabbed me and yanked me off the road. When I looked around, I saw he had saved me from falling into a big hole.

"Thanks," I said, flustered.

He looked proud of himself and reiterated his offer to take me anywhere I wanted for a dollar.

I shook my head again and motioned him away. I was trying to pour water on him, but it was just rolling off. He wasn't listening.

After walking another 100 feet, he grabbed me again and pulled me off the road seconds before a tuk-tuk whizzed by. It would have run me over!

Now I'm thinking this little guy saved my life twice, and I'm still being mean to him. He must have sensed I was softening.

"I get my tuk-tuk, and I take you for hours for one dollar," he said.

"You don't understand," I tried to explain once more. "I appreciate you looking after me but I'm not going anywhere with you alone."

"Oh no, we won't be alone," he replied. "I bring my friend! He works for me. He's guarding my tuk-tuk right now."

That sounded even worse – two against one.

"I know four places where you can get very good aspirin."

Just then, another tuk-tuk whizzed by, and he again pulled me out of the way. Okay, I thought, maybe trying to do this on my own wasn't such a good idea, and he did save my life three times. Maybe I'll try him out.

So I nodded, and he started smiling. We walked another four blocks, well past the original pharmacy, turned a corner, and there must have been a million tuk-tuks parked on the street. And sure enough, just as he had promised, his friend was protecting his tuk-tuk. I climbed in back, the little guy got in right next to me and, with his friend driving we set out. Traffic was so congested, I soon realized I couldn't even jump out if I had to; I'd instantly get hit by another vehicle. I was trapped, and I was almost down on the floor I was so scared.

The little guy noticed my anxiety and said, "You don't have to be afraid of his driving; he's been doing this for 20 years. He's a good driver and a good family man."

The little guy then directed his friend to a pharmacy where I was able to buy some aspirin. But there was a limit. For some reason they wouldn't sell me more than five tablets at a time. So we had to stop at four or five different pharmacies before I gave up. It was crazy. I couldn't believe it was for real.

"If there is anything else you want to buy, I know where to get it," the little guy said.

"I am looking for a sarong."

"I know just the place."

So we set off driving and driving, passing all these stores with sarongs in the windows, but none of them were good enough for him. I was starting to worry because we had probably traveled 10 miles. Then we stopped for gas. I figured this was how they get you; they'll ask me to pay for the gas. But the little guy paid. Noticing my continuing concern, he said, "I can prove to you I'm a good guy. I have references." And with that he handed me this little tablet filled with handwritten comments such as, "This was a wonderful trip," signed Joe Blow. Each page had something like this written on it. I'll never know if they were actual customers or just more of his friends.

When we finally arrived at the sarong shop, I found out – although I should have guessed – that it belonged to his cousin. I was about to carry my pharmacy bags in with me, but he told me to leave them in the tuk-tuk and his friend would watch them. I remember thinking: *It's only aspirin and if I lose it, I lose it.* So the little guy goes with me into the shop and starts looking around, saying "You don't want this one," looking some more, "Not this one" and then finally "This is the nicest one." And it really was! He even helped me negotiate the price. When we returned to the tuk-tuk, sure enough, the driver was still there, practically draped over my packages.

By this time, I'd been gone about six hours, and although I was more relaxed than I had been at the beginning, the ship was leaving that afternoon and it was time for me to get back on board. But I had forgotten the name of the hotel where the shuttle bus dropped me off. That terrified me because I didn't want them to know that and, if I had to run away, I wouldn't know where to run. So I had to think fast.

"One thing I haven't done yet is use the computer," I said. My plan was to email my daughter in the States and tell her where I was in case anything happened. The tuk-tuk did a U-turn in traffic, and they took me to an Internet cafe. When I went inside there were some other people from Crystal, and I was so happy to see them. I emailed my daughter, telling her I was on a tour alone in Thailand in case she never heard from me again. But I got the name of the hotel from the other Crystal guests and then told the little guy to take me there.

In the tuk-tuk again, traffic thicker than ever, he started telling me his life story. He said he had a wife and three children and made about $500 a year. Miraculously, none of them had been killed when the tsunami hit Phuket a year earlier. But he said they were forever changed. Each night he parked his tuk-tuk backward in the alley, so if another tsunami came and they had to quickly flee they could just jump in and go.

It was quite a sad story but I was getting more and more worried. I was looking for things that were familiar, but I wasn't seeing anything I recognized. It seemed like we had spent the whole day driving in circles, so I wasn't sure where we were. And the ship would be leaving shortly.

All of a sudden, we were back at the hotel, and I saw the Crystal shuttle. I was so relieved. Now remember the little guy had promised to do all this for a dollar, so when I asked him how much I owed him, I was surprised to hear him reply, "One dollar."

I couldn't believe it. So I gave him $20 and the driver $10. I don't think I've ever spent $30 so happily. There were times when I truly believed I was being kidnapped. When I got back to my stateroom, I turned on the TV and there was a warning about another possible tsunami in the next few days. I was so glad I had given the little guy and his friend some extra money in case they needed to evacuate. But, fortunately, another tsunami didn't hit.

Although I truly believe the world is basically a good place, that incident changed me. Even though I see women even older than me get off the ship alone in Third World ports all the time, I realize that it's no longer smart for me to do so. I hear stories all the time of people getting off the ship and falling and breaking their ankles or legs. Even in places you think would be safe, things can happen. One passenger was pickpocketed at the Vatican!

I'm at the point where I've been to most of the world's major ports 50 times. I don't need to see them again and take any chances. People are always asking me if I need anything, so if I'm out of lipstick or something, they'll get it for me.

I don't care if I'm in Cape Town or Rio, I prefer to just sit and do needlepoint up on the Lido.

AN ANNOUNCEMENT FROM SERENITY'S
CRUISE DIRECTOR RICK SPATH

Mama Lee is a wonderful lady. Here are a couple examples of her outlook on life. They're classic stories I even occasionally tell on stage:

A few years ago I was rejoining the Serenity in Lisbon after a couple months off. Mama Lee was there to greet me. She gave me a big hug and said, "I've missed you; it's great to have you back."

"I see you were in Casablanca last week," I replied. "How was it?"

Her response was: "WE WERE'???"

My point being, Mama Lee has absolutely no clue where the ship ever is, which I joke about with her on a daily basis. Although she often says she is aboard for the dancing, let it be known that she is here for the ship ambiance more than anything. She loves to be around people, do her needlepoint, and dance a little bit in the evening.

One morning I was sitting with her up at Tastes as she was doing her needlepoint. We were at a table on the starboard side of the ship. Tastes has a retractable glass roof, and rain was pelting quite heavily on it. You could also hear the wind blowing quite strongly outside. Mama Lee commented on how bad the weather was but said she was surprised how the ship was sailing without any movement.

I had to keep myself from laughing. "Lee," I finally said, 'In case you haven't noticed, we are docked in port today.' From where she was sitting, her view was of the open sea."

Chapter 19

SO MANY HANDSOME BOYFRIENDS

Since I love to dance, I've gotten very close to many of the Ambassador Hosts over the years. Some are like family to me. We stay in touch via email, and when they return to the ship, they hug and kiss me. Some I've known for 10 years. I dance with them every single day for weeks at a time. But I knew the day I lost my husband Mason, I would never replace him. It would be very hard to find anybody that good, and I didn't kid myself into thinking some other guy would just show up. I'm almost 90. There is no romance any more. The hosts are good friends and dancing partners, nothing else. They're all so strong and handsome! Why would I want to give all of them up for one old man I would eventually end up taking care of?

That doesn't mean I haven't had offers, mind you. Just the other day I had a passenger walk up and say, "Mama Lee, we've known each other for many years now, will you marry me?"

"I don't think your wife would like that," I said.

"Do we have to tell her?" he asked.

Believe it or not, I also get fan mail from people all over the world – some of them gentlemen – who write after reading about me in some newspaper or magazine. One fellow in Norway wrote a series of letters asking that I wire him $65,000 for hospital treatments and car repairs, not necessarily in that order. Another fellow in the Netherlands airmailed me an article about himself from a Dutch newspaper, plus some photos of windmills and oysters. Not sure what he was proposing there. But amongst the strange ones are also some nice notes like this from a woman I don't even know in Colorado:

Dear Mama Lee,

I read the article about you living on cruise ships since your dear husband became an angel. Way to go girl!

After my Father became an Angel, I did my best to keep my Mother active, taking her on trips and jaunts to Las Vegas until her health declined so much that she could no longer handle traveling. I am SO thrilled that you are "living life to the fullest!"

I never learned to dance and I know my Mother never did either. She suffered SO much the last 5 years of her life, the last 3½ in assisted living and nursing homes, going through everything she ever dreaded. She always wanted to go on an Alaskan cruise but I never succeeded in fulfilling that dream of hers, one of the many ways I failed her. Mom would have turned 95 this coming 12 May.

I am so thrilled for you! And to have family that loves you, Wow!

Keep on dancing young lady, keep on dancing.

Shirley

So as you can see, I have many friends on and off the ship. The Serenity, like most cruise ships, has its own photo department. There's a team of photographers who take pictures of everyone as they embark, go ashore in port, and celebrate at dinners and special parties during the cruise. Then they sell them to you. My albums are filled with photos of me with various officers at parties in the captain's quarters, at special celebrations for milestones (like my 100th and 200th cruises), and with the different hosts I dance with. I usually buy these photos at the end of each cruise and give some to the officers and hosts and paste the rest in an album. I enjoy looking through them and reminiscing.

I'd like you to meet some of the Ambassador Hosts, so I asked a few to jot down some memories of special times we had together. Call them Toasts from My Favorite Hosts:

MO ABDEL-GHANY

I've known Mama Lee longer than any other host. I met her on the Prinsendam, where she was always the first one on the dance floor and the last one to leave. She was also the first woman I ever met who lived on a ship fulltime. She still has a very good ear for music even though she's not as agile as she was back then. She has the ability to follow any dance host, even the mediocre ones, which works in her favor.

When I met her in 1997, I was teaching ballroom dancing at the University of Alabama, where I was also a professor of consumer economics. I taught a ballroom dancing course at night, and students took it as an elective. Most cruise directors on Holland America knew I was a professional instructor, so they invited me to conduct the daily dance classes. Mama Lee would be the first to show up for these as well, and I'd often pick her to illustrate the lady's step.

One of her good characteristics is that she's very humble. Although everybody knew she must be wealthy, she showed none of that to the hosts. And as the years went by, she adopted many of the hosts as part of her family.

Back then dance hosts came to Holland America and other cruise lines through agencies such as Six Stars and To Sea With Z (the first initial of the lady running the company). Some agencies were more interested in receiving the placement fees from hosts than examining the quality of their dancing or their character. This created a lot of problems. One time, four hosts were expelled from the Prinsendam for poor behavior and not dancing as much with the ladies as they should have been. Three were guilty, but one was innocent and became a casualty of the situation. They were not even issued plane tickets home. Mama Lee felt very sorry for the innocent one, and since this occurred in Ft. Lauderdale near where her family lived, she took him home and helped make flight arrangements.

On another occasion, one of the hosts was an impersonator. He had no clue about ballroom dancing; maybe he knew three steps in the swing. That particular segment there were seven ladies who were "followers" of mine, meaning they came on that particular cruise to dance with me. (I send them my itinerary, and they follow me; it's not uncommon among top-notch dance hosts.) These women were very good dancers, and this guy was scared to dance with them. Since

Mama Lee has a very calm demeanor, he ran immediately to her for help. He'd ask her, "What's this music? What type of dance? Is this a rhumba? Can you teach me?" Some of these women can be very mean to hosts who don't know what they're doing, and this fellow sought refuge with Mama Lee. She was very patient and helped him as much as she could. Sometimes she just stood there while he shuffled his feet. That was okay with her.

One of my most embarrassing moments dancing at sea, although I did not realize it at the time, involved a gorgeous lady on the Prinsendam. She sat by herself every night observing the dancing. All the ladies were curious about her because she was so beautiful, but she politely refused their invitations to join them. Since I taught the dance classes, she must have felt a bit more secure approaching me because one day she asked if I would teach her to dance. She was much taller than me and very well endowed. So let's just say, I really enjoyed the experience.

About three years later I ran into Mama Lee, and she said, "Mo, did you know that gorgeous woman you were dancing with was a man?" I couldn't believe it. She was magnificent! Mama Lee went on to explain that the woman had been called into the cruise director's office because there was some confusion over her travel documents. Evidently, the previous year while cruising on the Prinsendam she had indicated she was male but now this time she was female. In the interim, she'd had a sex-change operation. The only giveaway, Mama Lee added, was the fact that she always wore a scarf around her neck to hide her Adam's apple. I must confess that really took me by surprise!

Another part of a host's job, although not required, is to escort ladies when in port. Many will not go off the ship otherwise. A few years ago, I escorted Mama Lee in Sydney, Australia. We went to the Botanical Gardens, which was within walking distance of the dock. We enjoyed all the different trees and flowers. And on another occasion, I escorted her in Venice. She stopped in all the shops, mainly to look at earrings. As the years go by, though, I've noticed she's less interested in going out. She's seen all the ports. Sometimes she doesn't even know what port she's in, and that's not because she isn't on top of things. Her destination is the ship. She's here for the environment and the dancing. At her age, there's no way she would be going to a club and dancing if she were on land. The ship is her haven. It provides an environment where she can feel protected. That's especially important in today's crazy world. People attack other people on the street, there are all types of financial schemes that older folks fall for, so the feeling of security she has here is very important and helps keep her vital.

She also has a support network on the ship. I remember when her daughter passed away, almost every one of the dance hosts sent her a message of sympathy, regardless of where they were in the world. Over the years, she has become our godmother. When we have a problem dealing with some of the ladies, we know we can ask her for advice. And likewise, if she doesn't like something or sees a situation developing, she'll let us know. She's a special lady.

My Two Cents (Mama Lee): The best thing about writing a book is that you always get the last word! That's a really funny story about Mo and the gorgeous man/lady on the Prinsendam. She was not only beautiful, with legs a mile and a half long, but she was also very mysterious. The women who dance regularly always sit together, but she sat by herself. She knew South American dancing but not ballroom dancing, so Mo was teaching her. People would come in the evening just to watch her dance. She was a delight to look at; everything was where it should be. She was about a head-and-a-half taller than Mo, so his nose was always in her cleavage. It reminded me of a set of windshield wipers. He was really enjoying his location.

When you live on a ship, you are privy to all the gossip. As the cruise was ending, I heard this woman had been called into a private room because immigration had come on board. They sent for her and asked her to explain why her passport listed her as female when just a few years earlier she was male. That's why she was so perfect; she had been completely reconstructed!

Well, a few years later, I saw Mo and told him this story. I thought he was going to faint. But hindsight is always 20-20. He, too, remembered the colorful scarf she always wore around her neck to cover her Adam's apple.

HAMID MANSORY

I was dance hosting on the Prinsendam when Mama Lee was living there. I had known her for about three years. She was always very respectful to the hosts and liked my lead, so we danced a lot. On one particular Caribbean cruise, we really had some monkey dance hosts. There was no management or supervision, and they took advantage of it. One guy was eating figs from his pocket while he was dancing. Another host didn't dance for two weeks because he said he broke his toe. And a third guy was skipping dance sessions because he said he had a cough. I went to the cruise director and told him I couldn't work like this. Rather than take action himself, he told me to bring everybody to his office. So I suddenly became the bad guy for reporting them, and I made three enemies. But as a result of that meeting, a miracle happened. The broken toe healed, and the cough disappeared. But the monkey business continued.

One of these hosts was also running around with some of the women, which is forbidden. I had one woman crying and shaking in my arms saying, "He dumped me for that one." Well, all this got back to the cruise director, who called in Mama Lee because he knew she was very aware of everything. She told him we were acting like monkeys. We ended up getting called before the captain and dismissed when the ship got to Ft. Lauderdale. This was not the end of the cruise, so none of us had plane tickets home. We were on our own.

Mama Lee knew I was innocent and had been doing my job (although I wish she had specified that to the captain), so because it was so difficult and expensive to find a flight home that day, she invited me to stay with her family. We had been at sea about two weeks, and Mama Lee's children had arranged a special Mother's Day celebration for her. But she called her daughter, Cathy, and explained my situation, and they were all real nice and friendly. Cathy had terminal cancer at the time, but she went on-line (because I was very new to computers) and helped me find a flight the next day. It left very early, but she got up and drove me to the airport. I will never forget all they did. Mama Lee really feels for us hosts and, as this experience shows, even takes care of us. I am also from Iran originally. That might matter to some people, but not to Mama Lee.

After that incident, I could not host on Holland America anymore. In fact, they did away with their fulltime dance-host program shortly afterward, which is when Mama Lee moved to Crystal. When I heard her daughter had died, I sent my condolences, we emailed back and forth for a while, and she told me I should apply to Crystal. I did, she put in a good word for me with the cruise director, and I have been hosting there ever since.

Mama Lee is very smart. Living in a nice retirement home versus living on the ship probably costs about the same. But by choosing the latter, she has interesting new guests to share her dining table with every few weeks, and she gets to dance as often as she wants, not to mention see the world. She also gets a lot of attention from management, the cruise director and the staff. They are all very friendly toward her. I read articles about how interacting with negative, depressed and very old people can make you behave the same way. But everyone on the ship is younger, happy and having a great time, and that energy rubs off on her

Because she has lived on ships so long, Mama Lee has become a celebrity. Women who come aboard who are new to the ship ask me all the time about her – "Where is the woman who lives here?" Mama Lee takes pride in having such a unique lifestyle. And every time I come on board, it's like I have a mother here waiting. She welcomes me, gives me a hug, and asks how I've been. I tell everybody if you can afford it, why not live this way, too?

My Two Cents (Mama Lee): I'll never forget that cruise. The captain said, "I'm sick to death of you guys [hosts] and get off my ship!" But Hamid did not belong in that group and, he's right, I should have spoke up on his behalf. I don't know what I was thinking. It was three hosts making all the trouble, not him. They not only deserved to be thrown off the ship but also into the ocean!

One night, five ladies were sitting on the couch waiting to dance but none of those guys would get up to ask them. I had been dancing with Hamid, and we went up to them at the end of the set. I said, "What the hell are you thinking? There were five women sitting there in a row!" The host in the middle, a very short guy, pointed to the hosts on either side of him and said, "If they're not working, I'm not working."

Well, two wrongs don't make a right.

The little guy in the middle had his legs crossed, and as he uncrossed them he kicked Hamid. Hamid kicked him back, and the guy started screaming, "Help me, I'm being attacked!" Hamid slapped his hand over the guy's mouth to keep him quiet. People walking by couldn't believe it. You should have heard the stories that came from that episode. Even people who weren't there knew everything.

When Hamid was ordered off the ship, I knew I couldn't let this happen to him. He had no money or ticket, so I said come home with me. My daughter was actually in critical condition at the time, but she helped him save $150 by booking a flight on-line and then got out of bed and drove him to the airport the next day.

This also marked the beginning of the end for me living on the Prinsendam. It wasn't the hosts who were punished, it were the women left on board with no men to dance with.

JIM BATTAGLIA

I first met Mama Lee in 2010 when she was living on the Serenity. By chance I was seated at her table in the dining room. We bonded right away. My mother passed away in 2003, and Mama Lee became like a second mother to me. She's so comfortable to be with; I can talk to her about anything. When I'm at her table, I always finish her meals. She'll email me when I'm not on the ship and write, "Jim, I'm putting on weight because you're not here!"

She likes costume jewelry and whenever we're in a port such as Istanbul or Kusadasi or Venice, where there's good shopping, I'll escort her into town. She loves to bargain. The vendors attack us. We say, "No, no." They say, "Yes, yes." It's fun.

But my favorite thing to do with Mama Lee is take her to movies on the ship. There's a theater aboard that shows a different film every day. For me, it's like a sleeping pill. I always fall asleep the minute I sit down in there. She kids me about that.

When I met Mama Lee it was my first time hosting on Crystal and, let me tell you, I was green. I hadn't even been on a cruise ship until just a few years earlier in 1999. After I retired from my job as a recreational therapist, I Googled "retirement jobs" and "working vacations," and "dance hosting" came up. I had no idea what it was. I contacted the agency that hired hosts for Cunard and found out you needed to know six basic dances, of which I already knew four. So I took classes in the rhumba and fox trot, auditioned, and got the job. I joined the ship on December 28, 2005 and went on to work for Holland America, Celebrity and eventually Crystal. Now I'm on ships between four and six months a year. Mama Lee keeps my tuxedo and other "work clothes" in her closet while I'm gone. That makes it easy for me.

When my sister and I were kids we took tap-dance lessons. We were basically the entertainment when my mother and father had guests over. My father used to say, "Dance or go to bed." When I became a host, I needed some business cards, so I thought that would make a clever motto. I handed those cards out for years with "Dance or go to bed" under my name. But when I came on Crystal and gave one to Mama Lee, she looked at it and said, "That's naughty. You better rethink that." I'd never thought of how it might translate!

Even more embarrassing, though, was the time I gave Mama Lee a copy of the movie *The Help*. Whenever I come on the ship I bring a bunch of DVDs to watch and usually share them with her and some of the other women. Well, unbeknownst to me there was a second movie in the sleeve. Let's just say it was "gay adult" in nature. The next time I saw her, she handed the movie back, and I asked if she liked it. Her eyes got real big, and she asked which one.

"Which one?" I said, not knowing what she was talking about.

"There was another one in there," she said handing them back to me, "and I watched that one, too."

When I saw what it was, I thought: *Thank God it was her and not some other woman I didn't know so well!*

So Mama Lee takes real good care of me. She's family. But I take care of her, too. The other night we had reservations at one of the specialty restaurants on Crystal. I'm waiting and waiting, and I finally think: *I bet she forgot.* So I go down to the main dining room and, sure enough, there she is at her regular table just finishing her salad. So I brought her upstairs, and she started all over again. But, like usual, I helped her finish her meal.

My Two Cents (Mama Lee): Let me tell you something. I never saw a man so speechless as when I returned that DVD he loaned me. Such a bad boy!

EMERY LENDVAY

Mama Lee doesn't go ashore too often any more, but she loves to shop in Turkey. We were in Kusadasi, just south of Istanbul, and I escorted her ashore. The souks (markets) are close to the port, and she likes to walk around. I was shopping for a leather coat – not dead certain I was going to buy one, but I wanted to have a look.

Mama Lee is not only a good shopper, but she is also a very good negotiator. So she had me try on this one jacket. It was very nice and real light; it folded into a small package for traveling. I liked it, but the guy wanted 1,500 euros, which was equivalent to $2,000 at the time. Mama Lee started negotiating, and after about an hour we eventually talked him down to $300. That was a very good deal, but then she asked him to throw in this $25 leather cap with a Ferrari emblem I'd been admiring. He grudgingly agreed. But I didn't have that kind of cash on me, so Mama Lee says, "Don't worry, I'll loan you the money," and I bought the coat and hat.

As we were walking out, both of us very pleased at how the day was going, she said, "Okay, now we go shop for a real Ferrari, and *you* do the bargaining!"

That's Mama Lee. She has a great sense of humor. She likes to tell new people she meets that she got rid of her house so now she's homeless. Whenever I hear her say that, I always add, "Don't feel sorry for her, have you seen her yacht?"

My Two Cents (Mama Lee): Emery is right. I am a hard negotiator. Here's how to work a great deal wherever you are in the world:

Give the impression you don't care if you buy it or not: If you let the storeowner know you really, really want something then he immediately has the upper hand.

Have a price in mind before you start negotiating: But don't share it.

Never accept the first offer: At most, counter-offer 50 percent less.

Walk out the door: I've done this more than once in some stores with the owner always running out after me.

Squeeze hard but not too hard: The other guy has to make a living too. I never go so far that I'm embarrassed walking away.

If something is selling for a buck or two, don't try to negotiate that: I see cruise passengers do this all the time, and it's ridiculous. These people have to eat, too.

DIRTY DANCING WITH CURTIS

No discussion of my favorite boyfriends would be complete without a mention of Curtis Collins, the professional dancer on board Serenity since 2001. I dance with Curtis at every party. He's wonderful.

Once he had on this new jacket and while we were dancing, as he twirled away from me, I noticed there were some strings hanging off the back. Afterward, I volunteered to go back to my room and get my scissors to cut them off. After all, it was a new jacket that he'd paid a lot of money for, and I'd didn't want people noticing strings hanging back there. Well, I thought he was going to have a heart attack. He said, "Mama Lee, those are intentional. I paid extra for them."

I don't know why anyone would do that to such a beautiful jacket, but I guess that's the fashion now.

Another time I was at a formal dance with him, and he asked me to feel the texture on another new jacket he had just got. "What do you think?" he asked.

"It looks lovely," I told him, "but it feels like Brillo."

Now he calls it his "Brillo jacket," and he says whenever he puts it on he thinks of me.

My favorite Curtis story happened one night when we were dancing in the Crystal Cove. I forget the occasion, but he'd been doing a little imbibing and was feeling no pain. We were dancing and everything was fine, but then he started dirty dancing – making lots of quick turns and bumping and grinding. Pretty soon, I started smacking his bottom every time he spun around.

The Cove was packed, and I could hear people laughing. All the while, I'm thinking to myself: *Why me? There are all these beautiful women who adore him!* I was mortified, but at the same time I was having a really good time! I didn't know what to do with him.

The next day I was up by the pool and Curtis came walking by. He said, "Thanks for the dance last night."

"I didn't think you would remember it."

"Mama Lee," he replied, "I will never forget it."

From then on anytime Curtis asks me to dance I always say, "Are you going to behave?"

And he says, "Absolutely not."

And I say, "Good."

And then we dance.

Chapter 20

THEY DON'T CALL ME 'MAMA' FOR NOTHING

The crew is wonderful on this ship. They watch out for me and really take care of me. And over the years I've gotten close to many of them. They're like my children – all 650 of them! And they often come to me for advice.

There's always a professional dance couple on board to give performances, lessons, and oversee the Ambassador Hosts. I became friendly with one half of one of these couples, and one night after the late dance set she asked if she could talk to me privately. It was around midnight so I invited her back to my stateroom. It turned out she was having a problem with her dance partner/boyfriend (not Curtis). She had picked up his phone by mistake, started pushing buttons, and found all these women he was in touch with. It broke her heart, and she was very upset. They had been talking about getting married, and here he was having all these relationships behind her back. She cried and carried on until 3 a.m. I gave her a lot of advice, because they don't call me "Mama" for nothing. She left feeling better, and things eventually worked out.

Shipboard romances happen all the time among the crew, and since this is a very small town, everyone knows everything. There was a waiter in Prego, one of the specialty restaurants on board, who was dating my stateroom attendant. Whenever I ate in Prego, he would slip me a note to give to her. I enjoyed that – running love notes back and forth.

Sometimes, though, things don't work out. Crewmembers fall in love on the ship and then when their contracts are up and they go off together they realize it's a very different world out there. It's even tough on me when they split up. And others are away from their spouses and children for months at a time while they're working on the ship. They often tell me about them and show me photos. They make me feel like I'm part of their families.

Certain crewmembers really stand out. For example, I always sit at the same table in the dining room. My favorite waitress is from Eastern Europe. She has a very strong personality and a name with hardly any vowels in it. I'll look at the menu and say, "I think I'll have this." She'll shake her head and say, "No you won't; you'll have this." And you know what? She's always right. She automatically gives me double portions of what I like (caviar!) and even cuts up my meat like I'm a three-year-old. I've learned not to argue with her.

If I'm a little late and someone accidently sits in my seat, she just about dumps the person on the floor. "That's Mama Lee's seat," she tells them. She's very loyal and protective. Every single night she helps me up from the table after dinner and walks me to the elevator. She's my personal escort out. One evening, just before she left to go home for vacation, I was running late. I sat down after everyone had already ordered and she said, "I didn't want to hold up the table so I ordered for you."

She's become my mother.

I had an Indian waiter at my table once. He looked like he was fresh out of high school, one of the youngest crewmembers on the ship. He was an assistant waiter, the bread boy actually, which is the bottom level in the dining room. He was like Peck's Bad Boy. Everything he did shocked you. He'd seat me at my table and then two minutes later he'd tap on my shoulder. I'd turn around, he'd say something to me, then when I turned back all my silverware was turned upside-down. I don't know how he did it because I never once caught him.

Another time I was in line at the lunch buffet with my plate in front of me. I set it down and grabbed one of those big spoons to get something else. When I went to put the food on my plate, my plate was gone. I had just filled it up two seconds ago and now it had disappeared. I knew immediately who was in the room. I turned around and, sure enough, there he was with my plate and a mischievous smile.

Whenever I had it up to my neck with this boy's nonsense, I'd say, "If you don't stop this I'm going to tell your mother."

"You don't have to tell her anything," he'd reply. "She already knows."

Another day he came galloping up to me. He was all excited to tell me he'd just been promoted to waiter. But he was getting moved to another table in the dining room. I said, "You understand you'll have to behave yourself now? Not everyone will put up with what you do."

"But that doesn't mean I have to behave myself with you, does it?" he replied, smiling.

One evening I was having dinner with Rick Spath, one of the cruise directors on Serenity. We were sitting on the other side of the dining room at a table for two by the window. All of a sudden, the boy shows up from the opposite side of the room and says, "Is there anything going on at this table between the two of you that I should be aware of?" Rick was hysterical.

Even though the boy specialized in high school humor, he added so much. He was always a great break in the day. And he continued working his way up the ladder. He'd always tell me when he'd gotten another promotion. Each time I'd warn him that he couldn't keep doing those things.

One day he came running and said, "Guess what? I've been named a butler." He was so proud, and I was so happy for him, but once again I told him to be careful. Those people up there in the penthouses don't take kindly to nonsense. As usual, he nodded and said, "But that doesn't mean I have to behave myself with you, does it?"

Well, he was a butler for a few years and all of a sudden one day he was gone. I tried to find out what happened to him, but I never did. I suspect he overdid it in the wrong place, and they let him go just as I'd predicted.

The stateroom attendants are also very sweet. These girls work very hard cleaning everyone's room twice per day. I had an attendant once who was new, and every day she forgot something in my room. One day it was a dirty rag on the couch, the next it was a bottle of disinfectant in the bathroom. Every day, she left something behind.

I happened to be in my room when the head housekeeper stopped by with her clipboard. She was checking that all the attendants on the floor were doing a good job. She asked how this girl was doing, and I said she was forgetful. I didn't intend to complain or get her in trouble, because it was really nothing, but the head house-keeper pulled it out of me.

"Oh no," she said, "I'll have to train her more."

Well, the next day the girl showed up on the verge of tears and started apologizing. I settled her down and made sure she understood I didn't file a complaint or report her. That made her feel better and she kept thanking me. But when she finally left, guess what she forgot? Yup, another bottle of disinfectant! Imagine being so sad and apologetic about making a mistake, then immediately making the same mistake again!

Needless to say, she didn't last long.

Chapter 21

MY POSSE AND ME

O ver the years that I've lived at sea I've made lots of lady friends. Norma Wilkinson is one of the best. I'm very close to Norma. She's from Winnsboro, Texas, and talks with the most delightful accent. Whenever she's aboard, I enjoy sitting with her in the Lido. I do my needlepoint, she reads, and we chat. But we have the most fun critiquing the people who walk by. There are so many characters, and it's quite entertaining.

"That woman is wearing a wig," Norma will say.

"I believe she is and, you know, it's doesn't look half bad," I'll reply.

Or...

"That man walks like a pigeon."

Or...

"Can you believe she's actually wearing that in public?"

Oh, we can be bad. But like I said, it's great fun.

Norma is a former English literature teacher, and she still does a lot of reading. One day, out of the blue, she said to me while we were sitting up in the Lido, "Did you know there are different levels of being a bitch?"

I said, "Norma, what are you talking about?"

She told me she was reading this novel that discussed different levels of bitchery. I'd never heard anything like that before and didn't know what to say, so I just went back to my needlepoint.

"Look at her," said Norma.

"Oh my goodness," I said. "Is she aware everyone can see her underwear right through that thing?"

Norma laughed and said, "You know, we're pretty good at this. We should write a column in *Reflections* [the ship's daily newsletter] with all of our observations."

"That's a good idea."

"But we would need a catchy title," Norma said.

"How about Nosey Bitches," I suggested.

Norma couldn't stop laughing at that.

Norma and I have been friends for almost 10 years. We met on her first Crystal cruise shortly after I started living on Serenity. She loves to dance. I love to dance. So our paths naturally crossed in the Palm Court, where there's dancing every evening.

She does three or four cruises by herself every year, so we see each other regularly. One time, she mentioned she had been wait-listed for an upcoming cruise. I think it might have been one of those big-band cruises that are always so popular with the dancers, so I told her to get off the wait list and just stay in my room. She was really surprised, but I told her to contact my travel agent and she would set it all up. Now whenever she comes on board, she's my roommate.

Now that I'm getting older I don't get off the ship much. It has gotten harder and harder for me to get around in these ports. The walking is never good with all the potholes, steps and cobblestones. But when Norma is aboard she usually arranges some kind of special outing. We went to see those statues on Easter Island, and one time I'll never forget we went shopping in Portugal.

As soon as we got out the door of the port building in Lisbon, this young man came over to us. He said, "I'd like to take you on a tour in my cab." Of course, we both kept walking, but he said, "I can take you anywhere you would like to go." We kept trying to ignore him, but he was so persistent and there was something so nice about him that we finally agreed to a short ride.

So we got in the cab, he introduced himself as Carlos, and I told him I needed a pair of shoes. He asked what kind and I described them – nothing with a heel, just some dressy flats. Well, he started driving. I was sitting in the front and Norma was in back. Soon we were in a section of town where the roads were very steep and so narrow he had to get out and tuck in the mirrors. He parked on this big hill outside a store with lots of shoes in the window and said, "Wait here, I don't want you walking around if you don't have to. We'll go see if there's anything nice." And before I could argue he left and Norma went with him. I was sitting in the cab on a road going straight up thinking if the brake didn't hold I was going straight down very fast. I was very nervous, alone in a strange town with strange people at a 45-degree angle.

Finally, he and Norma came back and said they didn't find anything I would like, but Carlos knew another place that might. So he drove us to another shoe store. This went on for a while, and I never did buy any shoes that day. Eventually he asked, "What else do you need?" and I said, "Let's look at dresses." So we headed for a store, and I found a dress I wanted to try on. Norma was off shopping in another part of the store and Carlos was wandering around, so I asked the shop girl where the dressing room was. She took me over to it, and I went inside and closed the curtains. As I was taking off my dress, it got stuck. I couldn't get out of my dress! My arms were stuck overhead and I couldn't see anything. Thinking the girl was right outside I called for help. I heard the curtain being pulled back and felt somebody lifting my dress off. When I looked up, it was *him* – Carlos! But he looked as unconcerned as anyone I'd seen. I'd never heard of a cab driver walking into a ladies dressing room and being so comfortable.

"You look like you know what you're doing," I said.

"I used to work in a dress shop and a shoe shop," he replied.

After all the shopping, Carlos asked when we were leaving. I told him Norma was flying home tomorrow but I had one more day in Lisbon before the ship departed. He said if I wanted to do more shopping I could stay overnight at his house so we could get an early start the next morning! That was very generous of him, but of course I wasn't about to do that. But we took him out to eat, and he was an absolute delight. We had such fun with him that day. He was like one of the girls. Norma whispered to me on the way back to the ship in the cab that we should find a way to smuggle him home.

Norma left the next morning, and I actually had a second day with Carlos. I don't remember what we did; he was just very comfortable to be with. After he dropped me off, I was up in the Lido later in the day and a waiter came over. He had a message for me and, lo and behold, it was from Carlos!

"I wish you Bon Voyage," it said.

"How did you find Carlos?" I asked the waiter.

"When you got out of his cab, I got in."

What a cab driver! I always look for him when I'm in Lisbon.

One last story about Norma: Not long ago, she and two of my other good friends – Carol Mills from Vancouver and Joanne Hennessy from Boston – were coming on the ship. Over the years we've cruised together many times – so much so that they call themselves "Mama Lee's Posse." Carol would always say before we went somewhere "Is the posse all here?" and the name stuck.

Well, unbeknownst to me, Carol came up with the idea of having T-shirts made with "Mama Lee's Posse" on the front and two tango dancers on the back. Norma designed them and had them printed at some place near where she lives that specializes in custom work. I was so surprised when all the girls turned up wearing them. They're black with white lettering – very nicely done. Of course, mine just says "Mama Lee." When everyone's aboard we have so much fun wearing the shirts. They're always the biggest hit. People stop us in the hall to take our photo.

Imagine that, I have a Posse!

And, as fate would have it, this Posse would lead me to a whole new chapter in my life....

Chapter 22

PERRY GRANT: MY CARY GRANT

In June 2016 I met an entertainer named Perry Grant. Since then he has become an overpowering influence in my life. I don't know what the hell happened to me. I truly feel I've found a soul mate. We think the same. We each know what the other is going to say before it's said. We have an unusual, uncanny understanding of each other. And whenever he's aboard, we're together every single day. My whole routine changes; I even skip dancing!

But look at me. I'm getting ahead of my story. So the Posse came aboard, and they said they wanted to take me to see this entertainer. He was new to Crystal and performed every night in the Avenue Saloon. Now I'm not a drinker nor am I a bar hound. In all my years on Serenity I don't think I ever set foot in the Avenue Saloon. Why would I want to sit in some bar when I could be on the dance floor? But the girls kept after me. They said he was wonderful, he'd been entertaining for more than 40 years, and he even had a place in Ft. Lauderdale, near where I used to live.

They insisted and insisted, but I resisted and resisted. I've seen thousands of acts on ships over the years. How good could this guy be? Finally, I gave in and agreed to take a quick look. So one night after dinner the Posse and I went into the Avenue Saloon. As soon as Perry saw me he said into the microphone, "Mama Lee! I'm having my attorneys draw up the adoption papers!" Everyone laughed, and we sat down at a table way back in the corner.

Perry was behind the piano wearing a sport-coat covered in big pink sequins. He was tall, pleasant looking, a blonde by choice, and extremely thin. He was under a light that made him glitter like Liberace. And he played for 3½ hours, one song after another, all the old favorites, always looking at the audience and never at a note of music. He sang well, played beautifully, and turned out to not only be a talented musician but also a very funny comedian. I found myself laughing and singing along. I couldn't take my eyes off him. He was fascinating.

At one point, Perry asked me to come up to the piano and turn on his little revolving disco ball. It's considered a big honor. While I was doing that he told everyone I was homeless but they should see my yacht, which got another big laugh. His show turned out to be great fun, and I ended up sitting through his entire performance and not getting to bed until nearly 2 a.m.

The next night I went back with the Posse, only this time we sat a little closer. Each night the place was packed. And Perry never took a break. It was amazing. One night I saw him drink seven bottles of water and a pot of tea and still not have to leave to pee. I got to thinking he must be part camel!

By the time the cruise ended and the girls went home, I was hooked. In fact, the first night I went into the Avenue by myself, one of the waiters came over and said Perry had reserved a special seat for me – the closest one to the piano. I've been sitting there ever since. The wait staff guards it like it belongs to the Queen of England. Now instead of dancing every night, which I thought I would do until the day I die, I'm sitting in the front row listening to Perry. The Posse had left, but I had a new habit. Some nights I'm out so late I don't wake up until noon the next day. It's exhausting.

Norma likes to tease me that whenever she leaves the ship, I always ask her to email when she gets home so I know she arrived safely. But this time before she left, she said, "I know you'll be busy with Perry so you don't have to write back." Well, I was very busy with Perry, and I never did reply to her email. Norma never lets me forget that she's the one who brought me to his show.

All this has been the strangest thing. I've been a widow for more than 20 years, and I've never felt like this about anybody since my Mason died. Nobody has ever gotten into my soul like this. Perry and I have a deep, deep understanding. But of course there can never be any romance. This will never go beyond friendship, but I'm fine with that. And I'm not the only woman who feels this way about Perry. He has a magnetic personality and a fan club of thousands. Some of them follow him around the world from ship to ship, and they've been doing it for years. One woman named Marcia signed up for an entire three-month World Cruise on Crystal because Perry was playing. We made her a member of the Posse because we sat together at his show every night.

They call this effect being "Perryfied." When he's singing and looking directly at you, his eye contact can melt you into a puddle. After somebody posts a photo of Perry and me on Facebook I get comments from women all over the world saying they're jealous of me. I don't even know these women!

Somebody asked me the other day if I'm a Perry groupie and if, after all these years of living on Serenity, I was going to start following him on other ships. Even though he has invited me to do so, why would I want to? I hate flying and packing and unpacking, and there would be all those other women I'd have to share him with. I have no interest in leaving this ship, although when he goes I really miss him. When he's aboard I meet him every day around 4 o'clock. That's when he eats his dinner in the Lido (always salmon, he's a vegetarian). Then later I go to his show and afterward he walks me to the elevator. He takes such good care of me.

In some ports, he even takes me shopping. In Ketchikan, Alaska, we went to Wal-Mart. We were standing near the entrance to the store, and he suddenly disappeared. I assumed he had gone to the men's room, but he came back pushing a wheelchair for me to sit on. He is one of the most polite and considerate people I know. Every afternoon when he comes to the Lido to eat, he asks if there's anything he can get for me. I always say no, but he never stops asking. Another time in Bar Harbor, Maine, he said there was something he wanted to show me at the top of this hill. He was pushing me in a wheelchair, and you never heard such a funny routine in your life. He kept saying, "I'm never doing this again" or "You're on your own on the way down." At one point, I even offered to push him. It was a hysterical afternoon.

Perry even looks out for me while he's performing. I don't know how he does it, but he can play without ever taking his eyes off the audience. He must have thousands of songs in his head. His show is very interactive, too. He interviews members of the audience every night. If someone tries to leave, he asks, "Can you wait 11 more minutes?" And most people do!

Sometimes during his show, Perry tells everyone to turn to the person on the right and slowly walk their fingers up their left arm. One night the man sitting next to me was drunk and Perry noticed him feeling his way up my arm which, to tell you the truth, I didn't object to at all. But Perry stopped playing and said, "Don't touch Mama Lee!"

Well, why? Why am I any different? He doesn't miss a thing.

Another night it was getting very late, and I was getting pretty tired. I started thinking how I could slide out of there. (Since I'm right up front that's not an easy thing to do.) While he was playing he said to everyone, "Now look at Mama Lee, she's thinking, 'How the hell am I going to get out of here?'" I couldn't believe it. He read my mind!

Perry also jokes about himself a lot. Even though he's in his mid-50s – as old as my youngest child, by the way -- he says, "I'm almost 30 already." That always gets a big laugh. Then he says while looking at us, "Ladies, at your age, find a man. It doesn't matter what he looks like as long as he can drive at night and has a big bank account."

Perry does basically the same show every night, which some people don't like. But I love it. He mixes up the songs, and the audience interaction is never the same, so it's always entertaining. Plus, you should see the way he dresses. For the World Cruise, he brought 18 trunks filled with 70 to 80 jackets – all very sparkly and custom made by a woman in New Hampshire. He buys the material all over the world. He even has three pair of rhinestone shoes that are just magnificent.

The girls thought it would be fun to invite Perry to join the Posse, so with my approval, they sent him the following letter:

Dearest Perry,

We want to honor you with this cordial invitation to join the very exclusive, member-restricted, highbrow, posh, intelligent, stupendous, fantastic, and a wee-bit-silly "Mama Lee Posse."

Should you accept, your mission will be to protect and serve to the utmost of your ability. Our goal is to promote questionable, but tasteful, plots, shenanigans, intrigues, and entertaining mirth.

With admiration and awe,

Your faithful and loyal Crystal friends,

Norma, Joanne, and Carol

P.S. A brand new, tasteful, designer-original, limited edition T-shirt is waiting for you when you return to Serenity. Its understated elegance will be equally at home under a sequined jacket, on stage for a Crystal show, or even for a last-minute dash to Wal-Mart!

To which Perry promptly replied:

Dear Girls,

I would be very honored to join the "Mama Lee Posse" group and understand the exclusivity of it. Sadly, the T-shirt will have to be redesigned for an artist such as moi ... what you may consider tasteful and elegant is sadly lacking in sparkly sequins and glitter, which is essential if the T-shirt is to be worn by an international star/celebrity. I will "spark up" the T-shirt and then it will be worn with much pride and honor.... xxxx

To which the girls promptly replied:

Such eloquent prose, Perry Grant! Welcome to the very exclusive "Mama Lee Posse!" How thoughtless of us not to consider your worldwide fame and talent as an entertainer extraordinaire! Of course, it would be essential for you to add gaudy embellishment to such a simple garment so once again you can out-sparkle and out-shine our modest attire. We can't wait to see the result....

The girls can be so silly sometimes, but it's great to have Perry in the Posse. Now other people are asking if they can join. But I tell them I'm not in charge. All new inductees must be voted on at our board meetings. Norma says we should consider annual dues, so we can all cruise more.

When Perry's not on the ship, I really miss him, but he emails me every day. In fact, I have a son who stopped writing to me, because sometimes I'm not that good at responding, and started writing to Perry. "Tell mom this or that," he says, "and next time you see her don't take her anyplace that's not safe." And Perry answers him!

As I said at the outset, how does this kind of thing happen to a woman like me who is almost 90? All I know is that when Perry looks into my eyes and sings, *You Make Me Feel So Young*, I feel like I'm 50 all over again.

Chapter 23

PUMPKIN

Even with all my friends and all the activities and all the ports and all the attention and glamour that comes with living on a luxury cruise ship, I still get lonely, especially at night after the ship has gone to sleep. Some cruise lines keep a coffee shop open all night, but not Crystal. Unless you want to sit by yourself in one of the public areas, there's no place to go. I keep my television on in my stateroom to provide some company. It's usually tuned to the news or *Keeping Up Appearances,* a very funny BBC show. I've been doing that for years.

But recently I got a pet. Please keep this to yourself because Crystal does not allow pets on board unless it's a service animal, and mine is not. I was in Kusadasi, Turkey, in 2016. The ship stops there a number of times during its summer Mediterranean season, and I usually go ashore because it's easy to get around and I like the stores. Well, I happened to walk into this one shop, and there was a long counter with a row of sleeping cats. Every kind of cat you could imagine was curled up in a little bed, breathing quietly. I fell in love with this orange-and-white tabby kitten and was about to buy it when a woman I knew from the ship came into the store. I told her I was buying a cat, and she scoffed and said, "You don't need that." And I thought to myself: *She's right. I have an almost 10-year accumulation of things in my stateroom, and I don't need anything else – even if it is the cutest cat I ever saw.* So I didn't buy it.

The ship left Kusadasi that night and I went to sleep and dreamed about that cat being curled up in bed with me. The dream was so real that when I woke up in the morning I actually started searching for it. When I couldn't find it I was momentarily concerned and depressed.

Later that day I ran into Raphael Derkson, who directs the Crystal Showband. I've known Raphael for years, and I told him all about not buying the cat and then dreaming about it and being very disappointed. He said, "Mama Lee, you should have bought that cat. In one week we're going back to Kusadasi, and I'll go get it for you if you can tell me where it is." Fortunately, I'd gotten a card from the store, and I gave it to him.

So a week later, the ship was in Kusadasi again, but it was pouring down rain. I thought: *Well, that's the end of the shopping tour because Raphael has a bicycle that he rides to the moon and back whenever we're in port, and he's probably not going to be riding it today.* But the rain didn't faze him. He bought the cat and brought it back. I was thrilled. The cat was still at the store waiting for me!

I tried to pay Raphael but he said, "I'm not taking any money from you. In fact, I've been looking for the right present for you." About a year earlier he had asked if I could needlepoint a picture of his red 1961 Volkswagen Bus. It's totally restored, and it's his pride and joy. He gave me a tiny photo of it, and the art teacher on board was able to enlarge it and put it on needlepoint backing. It took me weeks to make it, and Raphael loved it. He has it hanging in his room on the ship.

So the whole thing was kind of meant to be, I guess, and the kitten is wonderful. We always had dogs and other pets around the house when I lived in Florida. But I could tell right away that this cat was going to be special. I named it Pumpkin because of its orange-and-white coloring.

The first time my stateroom attendant came into clean, she spotted the cat lying on the bed breathing and screamed. "I have never seen a live animal on the ship before," she said. I told her not to worry because this one was not going to cause any trouble.

The next day the ship's tailor came to my room because I needed some alterations made. I went into the bathroom to change clothes and when I came out he was almost in bed with Pumpkin. I said, "What are you doing in my bed?" And he said, "I swear I just saw this cat breathing."

Well, by now you may suspect that I've been pulling your leg. Pumpkin isn't a real cat. A company called Perfect Petzzz makes them, and they only cost about 40 bucks. They have a D battery inside, and when you turn it on the chest gently rises and falls as if it's breathing. It's very life-like and fools people all the time when I bring it up to the Lido. It's the best pet I've ever had. I don't have to feed it. It doesn't scratch the furniture. And it doesn't wet the rug. But the best part is that this cat is my companion and my confidant. I tell it everything. I have gotten more pleasure from this kitten – along with a lot of late-night comfort.

Chapter 24

THINGS I MISS MOST: MY GREAT-GRANDBABIES

People are always asking me if I ever get homesick, and the honest answer is no. The ship is my home. Sure I miss my family, but they all have their own busy lives to lead. They don't want me hanging around. And the friends that Mason and I used to have in Davie are all dead. If I were living at home I wouldn't have anyone to even call.

I do miss my three great-grandchildren, though. Mason, who was named after my late husband, is three years old already, and the twins (Nolan and Logan) just turned one.

The twins were actually born 13 weeks premature, so their survival was borderline for a while. But I never got the urge to fly home and be with their mother (my granddaughter), Alecia. I'm a nurse and I knew they were getting the best care in the world at a facility that specialized in premature infants. If I went home I would have just added to the confusion. I've been away for so long I'm a novelty in the family when I show up.

Most of my family still lives in the Ft. Lauderdale area, so whenever the ship docks there or in Miami they either come to see me or I go see them. It's always a special time.

Last summer I was particularly excited about seeing Nolan and Logan for the first time. As we were getting closer to Miami, I got a message from the front desk telling me I needed more pages in my passport, and that I had to go to the passport agency once we docked and have them put in. Well, I'd been to the passport agency before and you end up standing in line for at least 45 minutes. It's a total waste of time. I only had one day in Miami, and I wanted to see my babies! I was really annoyed.

I called the front desk and said, "Why didn't you tell me this earlier? We just spent the last three months in Europe; I could have gone to any of the U.S. agencies there. Why take time away from me now that is so precious?"

Believe me, I did nothing but complain all the way to Miami. But they wouldn't give in; they insisted I had to do it.

So we arrived and I got off the ship, and Crystal had a car waiting to take me to the passport agency. I bitched and moaned the whole way, telling them I was getting cheated out of baby time. The car pulled up to the curb and a man and a woman were standing there. One reached out, opened my door, and they introduced themselves as representatives from Crystal's Miami office. It turned out that Crystal's new office in Miami, which had been open for only two weeks, was in the same building as the passport agency. What a lucky break!

The man and woman escorted me in and even stood in line with me. They were very consoling and kept saying they were sorry and they understood, but this was important. We finally got up to the window, and I signed all the required forms. The fellow behind the desk took my passport and told me to come back at 2 p.m. to pick it up. Now it was already about 11 and the ship was leaving at 5, so that didn't leave much baby time.

I got all riled up again.

Then one of the Crystal reps stepped in and told me I didn't have to worry about coming back. If I signed an authorization paper, he could pick it up for me and take it back to the ship. I thought: *There really is a heaven!* I was so impressed. It was very good politics for Crystal to do that — yet another example of the extra things they do, not just for me, but also for all their guests. That's why they're the best-rated cruise line in the world.

So I finally got out of the passport agency and spent about four hours with my family. It was a big crowd that day. I saw all my great-grandbabies, although the twins slept just about the entire time. My boys even drove down from Ocala. Everybody wanted to tell me everything, and they all talked at once. By the time I got back to the ship I was exhausted. It took me three days to recover. I was glad when everything got back to normal.

Whenever I get together with my family like this, they all say, "You should come live with me." But I see through that. I would be a babysitter. I don't want that. I babysat all of them. I'm past that now. And I would never be treated at home like I am on the ship. I'm not that dumb. On the ship if I call the tailor, he's knocking on my door within the next five minutes. Everything is at my fingertips. At home, it would be, "I'm busy" or "I can't do that now." I am spoiled rotten, and I know it. This is a fairytale life I lead. I do what I want when I want if I want, and if I don't want to do it no one pressures me.

Like I said, I adore babies, but I'm the baby now.

Chapter 25

THINGS I MISS MOST: MY CATHY

My daughter died of cancer in 2012 at the age of 59. Let me tell you, losing a child, especially a treasure of a child like Cathy, is the worst thing that can happen to you. It's even worse than losing a husband.

Cathy was a nurse just like me. She was always very caring and loved being in charge, so nursing was the perfect career choice. I take credit for her becoming a nurse. When she was six years old, I took her to work with me one night. She'd been sick all day with an upset stomach, and I didn't want to leave her home alone. It was the night shift, and the patients were all asleep anyway. (I liked night-duty because I didn't have to give baths, serve meals, or deal with visitors. If a patient woke up during the night, he really needed you. To me, that's real nursing.)

So I mostly kept Cathy on my lap while I did my charts. She loved being the commander of any situation, and she sat there all night feeling like she was running the hospital. I could tell she was thrilled, and that experience planted the seed of her becoming a nurse. She never argued with me when I told people that; she agreed I probably did plant the seed. A similar thing happened with my son Jimmy. He went on a cruise to Nassau with us when he was 10. The ship's security people adopted him and allowed him to stand with them as the guests came and went at the gangway. Later in life he became a policeman.

Cathy was diagnosed with cancer in 2010. She hadn't been feeling well for about two years prior to that, but avoiding doctors is a tradition in our family and also very common among nurses. Finally, my granddaughter Alecia's firefighter/paramedic husband (Jordan) insisted she get checked out. He took her to the doctor's office, and they did a lot of tests. The ship happened to be in town when the results were ready so I went with Cathy to the doctor's office. The doctor was someone she had worked with for years at the hospital and respected tremendously. He pulled no punches. He said, "I've gone over all your tests. You have colon cancer, and it has metastasized. The bad news is this will not have a happy ending, but the good news is it will only take two to six months."

That may sound like a cruel way of putting it, but being nurses we appreciated the doctor's directness. We knew all about colon cancer because that's what Mason had died from. The disease was advanced, and it didn't look like Cathy would suffer long. She and I both accepted the diagnosis that day. We didn't try to argue the doctor out of it or go looking for second opinions.

But as it turned out, two years later Cathy was still waiting. It was terrible. She was in hospice four times. I offered to stop cruising and go home to stay with her at least 10 times, but she wouldn't have it. She'd always say, "Mom, when the rest of the family asks how I'm feeling, I can say 'Much better' and they believe me. But if I told you that, you'd know I was lying. I can tell them anything and they buy it, but that would never work with you. It would be harder for me watching you watching me."

Cathy did ask that I email her four times a day, and I did – for two years. No matter where I was in the world or what I was doing, I always took the time to do that. It helped Cathy and it helped me by keeping us connected. I did a lot of reminiscing about Cathy during those two years....

Like the time when ... Mason and I brought our second child, Billy, home from the hospital. Cathy was two. We pulled up in front of the house, I opened the car door, and she was standing there with her little arms stretched out. "Okay Mommy," she said, "I'll take my baby now." I'll never forget that. She was always very maternal, and she was born bossy – Miss Bossy. At the age of four I overheard her saying to little Billy, "Take your damn foot out of the door." I was shocked. I never used that word around the house and wondered where she'd picked it up. Another time, when she was five, I was chatting with my girlfriends in the living room and she was listening to every word. Finally, I told her to go play in her room, to which she said: "But Mommy, if I do that I won't be able to hear what you're saying." That was Cathy – always honest.

Or the time when ... Cathy was a senior in high school and she was dating a boy a year older than her. I loved him. He was such a nice boy, and they were a darling couple. Everyone assumed they would marry after Cathy graduated. They went to the prom together, and I made

Cathy's dress. When my children were growing up, it was much cheaper for me to make their clothes than buy them. Some girls wouldn't be caught dead in a prom dress their mother made. But Cathy wore it and when she came home I asked her how it went. She said the prom was a lot of fun and that she had the nicest dress in the whole room. That meant everything to me. Unfortunately, her relationship with this boy never worked out. He got cold feet after Cathy graduated and moved away. She was devastated. She did very little dating after that and never married. She told me one day, "If I can't have a marriage like you and Dad then I don't want one." That was Cathy – always very sweet.

Or the time when ... Cathy announced she needed to find an apartment because she had just turned 18 and should be living on her own. Well, I had never heard of such a thing, but if she wanted to find a place then I wasn't going to argue with her. I went on duty at the hospital that night and mentioned to another nurse that Cathy wanted to move out. She said she knew of an apartment in her building that had just become available. She said it was the best one in the whole complex. I told Cathy about it the next morning, and we went to see it that afternoon. She fell in love with everything about it, and I put a deposit on it that day. It was dumb luck. As soon as we closed, she moved in. Didn't even wait for any furniture. She slept on the floor, but she didn't care. She was so excited to have her own place. From then on things started leaving my house and showing up in hers. Once I was sitting on the couch in my living room, and I saw her go by carrying this big picture. I asked what she was doing, and she told me she needed it more than I did. Whenever I caught her taking something that was always her answer. Years later she told me she never thought I would allow her to get her own apartment. She expected me to give her a hard time. In fact, she joked that it happened so fast she felt like she had been thrown out. And although Cathy often visited, she never did spend another night in my house. That was Cathy – always very independent.

Or the time when ... Cathy decided to upgrade from her apartment to a full-size house. Mason and I had just purchased a fixer-upper in Davie that was about 50 years old. It had five bedrooms and was way more home than a single workingwoman needed, but Cathy told me she wanted a big house so all her nieces and nephews could spend the night. So we turned the place over to her. She put in a pool, and her brother built a huge deck. After Mason died and I sold my house, I lived there in between cruises. Cathy renovated one of the rooms for me. There was a sign on the door that said "Caution: Grandma's Cabin." Inside was a huge picture of the ocean on one wall, so I always had an ocean view. Only Cathy would think of that. She even squared off a corner of the room and made it into a walk-in closet for all my clothes. She was so considerate. And all my grandchildren did end up spending lots of time in that house. She actually raised two of them, Alecia and Billy, after their parents divorced. She was their Rock of Gibraltar, attending PTA meetings, Billy's wrestling practices, everything. That was Cathy – always taking care of everyone.

Or the time when ... Cathy befriended a woman named Sally. She was in her 80s, a feisty spitfire who had been a buyer for Neiman Marcus in New York City. She and her sister, Dora, who was also in her 80s, were moving to Florida and looking for an apartment. The bank Mason worked for was building a new headquarters, and he was in charge of operations. The first five stories would be bank offices and the rest would be apartments. He put hardhats on these little old ladies and gave them a tour. They immediately fell in love with the apartments and Mason. Now when I say Sally was feisty, I mean it. She had never driven a car before, but after she retired she bought herself one, got her license, and the two of them drove to Florida. We had just moved into our new place in Davie and were having a housewarming. Because they didn't know anybody in town, Mason invited them. They came and met the entire family, took pictures with everyone, and immediately adopted us. From then on, whenever anybody had a birthday they got a present from Sally and Neiman Marcus.

Years later, Mason heard Sally had been admitted to Golden Glades Regional Medical Center where Cathy worked. So he called and asked Cathy to stick her head in and say hello. Well, you tell Cathy that someone is sick or needs something, and she'll be there every day. And that's what happened. Every single day she stopped in to perk Sally up and see if she needed anything. Since her sister didn't drive, Cathy often brought her things from home. Eventually, Sally recovered enough to leave the hospital, but Cathy and her remained close friends.

At this time, Cathy often went on weekend cruises with Mason and I. We'd leave on Friday evening from Miami and be back by 8 a.m. on Monday. No matter where we went, in every port, Cathy bought a postcard and sent it to Sally. This went on for years; Sally loved traveling vicariously through Cathy. Sally even insisted on giving Cathy all her jewelry. She said she wasn't wearing it anymore and it was just sitting in a drawer. So she asked Cathy to wear it on her trips and send photos. It was really good stuff.

Eventually, Sally's sister died and then shortly after that Sally herself passed away. That's when Cathy found out that Sally had willed everything to her, including the apartment, several valuable antiques, stocks, and about $150,000 in cash. We were shocked. I remember Cathy saying, "I never expected anything; Sally was my friend." That was Cathy – always giving and expecting nothing.

Or the time when ... Cathy had a very close friend named Marilyn. She was a little older than Cathy and her supervisor at the hospital. Marilyn married a firefighter, and Mason, who was also a notary public, performed the ceremony by the lake outside our house. Marilyn and her husband went on to have two children, and Cathy became their second mother. She babysat them a lot and really loved those kids. When they were five or six, the family moved to Philadelphia. They put all their stuff in a trailer. Marilyn took one car and her husband took the other. And Cathy followed in her car all the way to Philly to help them unload and settle in and then she drove back. She would do anything for a friend. That was Cathy – always totally selfless.

Marilyn ended up taking a leave of absence from her job in Philly and moving in with Cathy, when Cathy became too sick to take care of herself. When I found out Marilyn had moved in, I knew it was getting close to the end. I was still corresponding with Cathy every day, but her emails were getting more and more confusing. When she aimed for one key, her finger always landed on the next key over. It took me a while to figure that out – it was like a coded letter – but I was able to read them. One particular email I'll never forget: She wrote: "I don't know why something that should be so easy is so hard. Every day I wake up and say, 'Oh no, I'm still here.'"

Marilyn emailed me every day, too. She'd tell me she didn't know what was keeping Cathy here or why she was hanging on. Then late one night while Marilyn was sitting in Cathy's room, Cathy suddenly sat up and started reaching around. She was obviously looking for something. When Marilyn asked what she was doing, Cathy said she was trying to answer the phone. Marilyn told her it had never rung, but Cathy insisted it would. Marilyn emailed me the next day saying she believed Cathy was waiting for a call from me.

Now I had already offered at least 10 times to come home to be with her, and Cathy had always refused. I had also asked her many times if she wanted me to call, but she'd always said, "Good heavens, no. It would be a wasted call. I would be crying. You would be crying. We wouldn't even be able to speak." I told Marilyn all this, but she kept insisting that even though Cathy wouldn't admit it and kept telling me no, she really wanted me to call. "She doesn't always tell the truth," she said.

So I didn't know what to do. I didn't want to upset Cathy and make her suffer more. I happened to mention all this to Gary Hunter, the other cruise director on the Serenity, and he said, "The heck with that, you have to call her." He dropped what he was doing and took me into his office, with me insisting this was going to be a wasted call and that everyone was going to start crying. He said, "If you can't talk to her, I will." So we called from Gary's office and Marilyn answered. She said, "Cathy, your mom's on the phone."

"My mom?"

"Yeah, she's right here, take the phone."

When she said hello, I knew the whole story. She was heavily medicated – on morphine to minimize her suffering – and I could barely understand her. I didn't want to remember her like that, so I said, "Give the phone back to Marilyn." I told Marilyn I seriously doubted she would remember I had called the next day.

Cathy died either later that same day or early the next. When I got the news that she was gone, I was relieved because she had wanted to die for so long and was in so much pain. Whether what happened at the end was a premonition, whether she wanted the phone to ring and hear my voice one last time, I don't know. We were always honest with each other, and I don't find any hidden meaning or solace in how it ended.

Cathy was cremated, and there was no funeral. There has never been a funeral in our family. My father was totally against them. He'd always say, "When I'm here I'm here and when I'm gone I'm gone. I don't want people coming to look at me when I can't see them." My mother felt the same way, and so did Mason and Cathy.

I had asked Cathy if she wanted me to come home after it was all over and she said, "What for? I won't be here."

And that was my Cathy – always the pragmatist.

Chapter 26

BEAUTY TIPS AND TATTOOED LADIES

Some people ask me if living like I do without any worries and breathing all the fresh sea air is the secret to staying young. Not having anything to worry about definitely helps, but I'm not outside very much. I needlepoint in the Lido all day, and my stateroom doesn't have a veranda. I'm inside the ship just about all the time.

I do go to the beauty shop on board once a month to have my hair done. (I set it myself every night.) Every two to three weeks I also go to have my nails done. If I had all the money back that I spent on nails over the last 50 years I could upgrade to a penthouse. I've had terrible nails my entire life, so having these long acrylic ones now is my one indulgence, although they do make using the phone and computer a lot more difficult. I make a lot of typos. Tutti-frutti is my favorite color because it goes with the clothes I like to wear, usually lots of purples and pinks.

I wear lipstick and a little makeup to cover up what needs to be covered up. The skin problems I have now come from years in the sun when I was younger. I stay out of the sun now. Other than that I don't alter a thing. I don't have any elaborate nighttime beauty routine or use any expensive creams, and I've never had any work done. Women who've had plastic surgery go through here all the time. I think plastic surgery causes more troubles than it solves. Their faces are tightened up so much their eyes bulge out, and they have no expressions. It's all very artificial looking.

Another thing I don't understand, especially with the younger women these days, is why they get these tattoos all over their bodies. I went to the Mozart Tea one afternoon in the Palm Court. It's a very fancy affair with the little sandwiches and pastries and the wait staff all dressed up in period costume. The waitresses wear these long dresses with scoop necklines. One girl had the bow of a ship emerging from her neckline. I couldn't believe it! I asked her what it was, and she said just one of her many tattoos. I don't approve of it at all. They're doing life-long damage to their skin that's not reversible and is only going to get worse with age. They don't realize how much everything droops later on.

One time, the Posse and I were talking by the pool and we saw this woman take off her cover-up by the hot tub. She was a senior lady, and she had this big tattoo on her back. Then her friend took off her cover-up, and she had two or three tattoos. Turns out there were five ladies in all, and each one had tattoos all over their shoulders and backs. I said to Norma, "We are way behind with the fashion."

So a few days later, Norma and Carol went ashore and, because the Posse's motto is "We're into shenanigans and downright silliness," they bought some temporary tattoos – roses, butterflies … things like that. They put them on their shoulders and went dancing. They tried to get me to do it, too, but I refused.

I am anti-tattoo.

Chapter 27

THE LAUNDRY THIEF

The vast majority of guests on the ship are trustworthy, but you still need to be careful. I used to do a lot of knitting in college. I moved to Florida with 28 sweaters and matching pairs of socks, but I didn't need them, so I gave up knitting and went 65 years without doing it. Then a few years ago I got friendly with the knitting instructor on board, and she talked me into coming to her class. I ended up buying a $50 kit for a beautiful mohair wrap. I made it, and it turned out gorgeous. I wore it to a movie in the Hollywood Theater one night. While I was sitting there for two hours it slid off my shoulders and into the back of the seat. Afterward, I went home, but the wrap stayed at the movies. When I got back to my stateroom and realized I'd left it behind, I ran back. But by the time I got there, it was gone, and I've never seen it since. Fifty bucks out the window, plus all that time to make it! Now I've definitely given up knitting for good.

But the best story of all —one that has become legendary on the ship – is the one involving the laundry thief. A couple of years ago, there was a woman on board who took a nice black dress of hers to the laundry room. There's one on each floor, and they're public. She just wanted to get the wrinkles out, so she put it in the dryer, set a timer, and went back to her room. When she returned the dress had disappeared. She checked Lost & Found. She asked the room attendants on the floor if they'd come across it. Nobody had seen it.

Now here's where things get interesting. The very next day, she's in the main dining room for dinner and sees her dress on another woman. Now this was a unique dress so there was no chance this was coincidence, so she walked over and confronted the thief.

"That's a very nice dress you're wearing," she said, "but it's my dress – the one you took out of the dryer last night!"

The thief smiled and very calmly said, "Prove it."

Now of course the woman couldn't prove it. There was no nametag in it. Even if she called security, what could they do? It's bad enough to have the nerve to steal a dress, but to have the gall to wear it in public the very next night when the owner would see it! That's just beyond me.

When I have to go into the laundry room, I do it at maybe two in the morning. It's safer and, besides, I don't like a crowd in there.

That reminds me of a story from when my son Billy was 10. He was going off to camp, and I spent two weeks sewing nametags into every shirt, pair of pants, piece of underwear, towels, sheets and socks that he was taking with him. I put it all in a duffel bag that was almost as big as he was and said, "Don't you leave anything at camp. Everything has your name on it. Make sure to gather it up and bring it all home."

Well, when it was time for him to come home, I went to pick him up at the bus stop, and there he was with his duffel and a big smile on his face. "Hi Mom," he said. "I didn't leave anything at camp."

"How do you know?" I asked.

Here the kid had never opened the bag, stayed in the same clothes, and slept on a bare mattress for two weeks. He was so proud of himself!

Chapter 28

WHAT ALL THIS COSTS ME

A few years ago, a freelance writer came on the ship to interview me about living at sea. He was a nice enough gentleman, and after we'd been talking for about 45 minutes he said, "I want to ask you a personal question. How much is this costing you?"

I told him I didn't want to answer that question and also tried to explain that no two people pay the same thing. It's all negotiated differently depending on what kind of stateroom you have, your length of stay, and many other things.

Well, he left the ship and sent in his article. His editor liked it, but he said he had to have a price or else he wouldn't publish it. So the writer made a figure up. He said I was paying an average of $450 per day, or about $164,000 per year. This is the same article I mentioned way back in Chapter 1 – the article that ended up being published all over the world. But that figure was way off.

I understand why people are curious. When I first started thinking about living on a ship, I wondered too. If you really want to know, here's what you should do: First, add up all your yearly living expenses – groceries, electric, insurance, maintenance, mortgage … everything. Then when you have a total figure, call your travel agent or Crystal's main office and ask how much it would cost if you moved onto a cruise ship. They'll tell you exactly what it'll cost. I remember when I added up all my yearly living expenses when I was in Davie, I was surprised at how much I was spending and how close that amount was to what I needed to live at sea. For me, it was almost an even trade.

Face it. None of the guests who regularly come on a luxury line like Crystal live in trailers. It costs them a lot to maintain their homes and their lifestyles. They could easily afford to do what I do if they wanted to. And don't forget, this is stress-free living, too, and you can't put a price on that.

So this is going to be a very short chapter.

It's none of your business how much this costs me.

Chapter 29

THIS CINDERELLA LIFE

I don't gamble. Well, I take that back. I did once. After dancing closed for the night, I was walking by the casino and I saw my friend pumping away at the slot machine. She gave me a quarter, I put it in the machine next to hers, pulled the handle, and it spit out $25. I've never gone back.

I guess you could say my entire life has been like that. Mason and I worked hard, but I'm also smart enough to realize I've been very lucky to have such a fairytale life. I ask myself all the time, "Why me?" I've never been able to figure it out.

People tell me I'm so courageous for selling my home and choosing to live on a cruise ship. But courage didn't have anything to do with my decision. I started cruising for two days, then three days, then five, seven ... it grew gradually. I decided to live at sea fulltime for selfish reasons. I hated flying and packing and unpacking. There's nothing special about me. Anybody who really wants to do this can do it, maybe not fulltime on Crystal, but there are lots of less-expensive cruise lines.

People also ask me all the time, "Don't you feel bad spending all that money that would go to your children?"

Hell no! I already do so much for them.

I did not write this book to try to convince other seniors to live on a ship or to start some new retirement trend. If they're not smart enough to discover this on their own, it's not my job to tell them. There are three other women living fulltime on the Crystal Serenity as I write this. There used to be a woman who lived on one of the Cunard ships for many years, but I think she's now either in a nursing home or dead. I've been living at sea fulltime for 12 years, nine of them with Crystal, so I just might hold the record.

This lifestyle suits me very well. I remember one 12-day land trip that Mason and I took through Europe. We had to get up every morning at six and be completely packed with all our bags in the hall so we could eat breakfast and be off for the day. Then we would land in another place and do it all over again the next morning. I hated it. I could never get out of bed so early. It got to the point where Mason wouldn't tell me what time it was when he woke up. He just said, "It's 20 minutes after." But he never said after *what*? I'm pretty sure that was the last land trip we ever took.

Even when I was a kid and my mother would be having a party and she'd tell me to go to bed, I resented that. When I became a nurse and opted for night duty, I'd call her and say, "I'm staying up all night, *you* go to bed." It did something to me as a child, feeling knocked out of the action, so I became a night person. Nobody tells me what to do on the ship, and I set my own schedule. And I'm always part of the action.

Crystal is building two new ships that will have residences on board, sort of like condos you can buy. I won't be purchasing one of those. My residence is right here with a crew of 650 who all know me. It's impossible to feel alone here. The other day I went into the Lido, and everyone was asking, "Where were you for lunch yesterday? Why didn't you come in?"

If I'm not somewhere I'm supposed to be they get worried. If I make an appointment in the spa (and I've been known to forget the occasional appointment because I really have no concept of what day it is out here), they know where to find me.

I don't believe in reincarnation, so I'm enjoying every minute of every day. I'm not going to wait. As a nurse, you learn a lot about life and its realities. I don't live in daydreams. Everybody dies. As a nurse, I was around death a lot. Everybody lives in fear of it, but it's not that big a deal.

Recently there was an elderly Japanese woman who died on the ship. She was traveling alone and loved to dance. She was in her stateroom, putting on her dancing shoes, anticipating going out for the evening to do what she enjoyed most, when she dropped dead.

Everybody should be that lucky.

AFTERWORD

HOW TO CRUISE THROUGH LIFE: MY 12 RULES

Travel as much as you can. It's the best way to learn, because you see things directly rather than reading about them in books or watching them on TV. Then you can form your own opinions.

Don't spend money on stuff you'll eventually throw out. When you don't want it anymore, you'll find out nobody else wants it either. Hang onto your money. It's just as rewarding to keep it and have it when you need it than to rush around spending it.

Be good, for goodness's sake. My husband, Mason, believed that if you're good all the time, you don't have to worry about the bad. That's why he wasn't religious. He thought most people just want to be seen at church; they're not really doing it for themselves. He believed you should be good for yourself.

Do your best today then try to do better tomorrow. This was another way Mason lived his life that I try to follow. He used to say the only man he answered to was the man in the mirror. If he could look him in the eye and say I tried to do my best today, but I'll try to do better tomorrow then everything will work out and you'll be successful.

Don't fear change. I gave up something I loved – nursing – to do something I knew nothing about – bookkeeping. But my new career turned out to be much more financially rewarding than my original one. Likewise, I didn't want to end up living alone or in some retirement home, so I got rid of everything I owned and decided to live at sea. Don't be afraid to try new things and do what makes you happy – provided it's not holding up a bank.

Realize when you're successful. In the rush to become successful, many people don't realize when they actually are. They're working so hard they miss it. Some never get to appreciate it.

Concentrate on the good things, not the bad. There was a woman at my dinner table the other night telling everybody how sick and tired she was of the way Crystal does things. Well, I took her aside afterward and said if it's really that bad, look for another ship, but in the meantime don't bring everybody else down at the table with your complaining. Rather than being insulted, she thanked me. She hadn't realized she was affecting the mood of the whole table. The older I get the more positive I try to be. Every day is a good day.

Be available to help other people whenever you can. Always try to put others first.

When it comes to love, trust your gut. You can't just label something true love. You have to know it, feel it. I knew very early on that Mason was the one for me. I never dated anyone else after I dated him, and neither did he. There was never any doubt in my mind. I told my mother shortly after I met him that when he decides to propose I'd be standing under the tree with a basket to catch the apple.

Be real. I'll never forget my mother giving a dinner party and putting out her best crystal. One woman she invited was very klutzy and broke two of the goblets. My mother was a very proper lady, and it was important to her that everything be just so. Every time this woman broke a glass, she just calmly went into the kitchen and replaced it. Finally, my father, who went to work some days with one black shoe and one brown shoe, left the table and came back with a can with the lid pried open. He filled it with water, put it down in front of her, and said, "Go for it." My mother could have died. But my father was real; he didn't worry about things like that. She concentrated on being a lady, and he concentrated on enjoying life. He didn't care what people thought or said and he never did anything for appearance. I'm more like Dad.

Focus on living not dying. I've outlived my mother, father, daughter, younger brother, husband and a lot of friends. I deal with loss by just going on. I concentrate on living not dying. I don't go to funerals. I try to enjoy every day, every year. And when my birthday rolls around again, and they tell me the number, I always think they're talking about somebody else.

Enjoy, enjoy, enjoy. If you hate it, why are you doing it?

Made in the USA
Las Vegas, NV
14 April 2023

70591889R10125